*Elegant*ENTREPRENEUR

Ten:Eleven Press

Elegant Entrepreneur:
The Female Founders Guide to Starting & Growing Your First Company
Danielle Tate

Copyeditor: Brin Stevens
Cover Design: Kim Smith
Cover Photo: Michael Ventura
Interior Design: Jillfrances Gray

First edition published December 15, 2015 in the United States by Ten:Eleven Press
ISBN 978-0-9970074-0-4

TO CULIN

*Thank you for awakening my entrepreneurial spirit
and making every adventure possible.*

TO MERRIC

*Thank you for your complete belief in me and for asking
each morning what my book word count was. I wrote this book
and you conquered handwriting. We did it!*

TO MY MOM

*Thank you for instilling a love of words and the power of writing into me.
I am an author because of you.*

~ TABLE OF CONTENTS ~

el·e·gant
> *adjective:* a pleasingly ingenious and simple solution to a problem.

en·tre·pre·neur
> *noun:* a person who organizes and manages any enterprise, especially a business, usually with considerable initiative and risk.

*Elegant*ENTREPRENEUR

~ INTRODUCTION ~

If you have a business idea and are considering starting your first company but don't know where to start, you are the woman I was a few years ago.

At age 25, I had just gotten married, was excelling in my sales career, and enjoying a comfortable life. But one day I had a business idea; an idea that stayed with me for weeks and kept growing in concept until there seemed no other choice but to pursue it.

With zero business background, I bootstrapped that idea into a business and grew it into a multimillion-dollar enterprise. My startup developed at the same dizzying pace as my learning curve. I wrote this book to tell you all the things I wish I had known before I founded a company.

This book will guide you through the steps to build a successful business, from idea to exit. It answers the important question: how do you make an idea produce money? It also discusses how to transform yourself into an entrepreneur—regardless of whether you have a business background or entrepreneurial ties.

Entrepreneurship is more than a job. It is an identity, a community, a lifestyle, and a mindset. Depending on your definition of success, it may also be the path to your ideal end goal. Unlike many positions along to-day's corporate ladder, entrepreneurship can deliver a lifestyle to support yourself and your family with flexibility, freedom, and satisfaction.

This book is divided into 12 chapters to represent the major steps to cre-ating a successful business (left brain) and 12 elegant entrepreneurship in-sights (right brain) that provide pleasingly ingenious and simple concepts to gracefully span the gaps between the business steps. These transparent, candid glimpses into the entrepreneur lifestyle will help you make a clear decision about whether the lifestyle is right for you and your vision of success.

Each chapter builds your understanding of business concepts. Key information helps you apply these concepts to your idea. Every chapter concludes with a summary of insights, an exploration of how it feels to be living that step, and suggestions for further reading on the topic.

Within these pages, over 25 female founders, entrepreneurs, and top ranking executives have shared their wisdom and experience. We hear from the founders of such companies as The Corcoran Group, Rent the Runway, Springboard Enterprises, ClassPass, WeddingWire, and MergeLane. Use their quotes, advice, and stories to avoid pitfalls and map your way to success. We are all cheering for you!

I wrote this book to fill a void—there are books written by female entrepreneurs, but very few fully-encompassing resources on how to build a business and become an entrepreneur. My goal is to not only help you find your place in the entrepreneurial world, but to enable you to flourish. Let's get started!

BEGIN ON THE PATH
TO ENTREPRENEURSHIP WITH
THE END IN MIND

What is your definition of success? Do you want to become the founder and CEO of a Fortune 500 company? Is your vision to change the world, revolutionize your industry, make a billion dollars, to be featured on the cover of Forbes magazine? Or is your goal to make money from your own achievements, quit your job, control your schedule, or simply have more time with your family?

The key to success is beginning with your ideal goals in mind, and then mapping the specific steps toward achieving those goals. Waking up each morning with your end vision burning in your brain will help steer your day, and your life. The more you visualize it, the more tangible it becomes. You are designing your own definition of success, and failure will soon not be an option for you. First, you must be completely honest about what success means to you; not success as defined by others. Focus your mindset on how to attain that end goal and allow yourself the flexibility to alter and adjust as life changes.

Do you already have an amazing idea for a business? Take time to plan your last step and your first step. Consider your goal with various perspectives—from mental telescope to microscope. Analyze potential outcomes and create multiple strategies to help grow your idea into a company. Don't be afraid to not know how you are getting from point (or step) B to point (or step) E. Understanding what you don't know and what you need to learn is part of the process. Then, again, consider: What is your end goal and the final step to achieve it? This is the last step on your map to success, and should be very easy to pinpoint because you've most likely been dreaming about it on a daily basis. Next, think about exactly what action or change is necessary to take you from where you are now, the first step on your journey, toward your goal.

The "race to success" is a misnomer. Racing implies a reckless dash, whereas many of the most successful people in life have strategically plotted their trajectories. Entrepreneurial women don't have to rush through what they hold important in life—such as love and parenthood—to achieve their goal. Instead, they stay focused on their goal by plotting and attaining the next two to three steps that will move them toward it.

I NEVER DREAMED
ABOUT SUCCESS.
I WORKED FOR IT.

~ ESTEE LAUDER ~

*Elegant*ENTREPRENEUR

~ Chapter 1 ~
# IDEA & INNOVATION GAUNTLET

There isn't a specific formula for generating those business-worthy ideas that launch successful startups. Most big ideas stem from personal pain or frustration. Entrepreneurs are professional problem solvers. They have identified something in our daily lives that could be made better and look for solutions. But they go beyond the average person, who is simply frustrated by an issue. Entrepreneurs investigate viable solutions and determine if those solutions have real business potential.

Ever heard the proverb "necessity is the mother of invention?" People facing problems for which no solution seems to exist are standing on the threshold of opportunity, whether they realize it or not. The majority of individuals do not bother or even consider daily problems in their lives, and instead elect to remain static and leave the world unchanged. A small minority search for and create what they need, ultimately realizing the opportunity to share their product or idea with the world. These are the budding entrepreneurs who will someday revolutionize their field and advance how we live day to day.

There are endless examples of women throughout history who have identified problems in their daily lives and, against all odds, found solutions, from Marion Donovan, who invented disposable diapers in the 1950s, to Sara Blakely, founder of Spanx. In fact, if you look at the top female-founded companies today, you will see the majority of these women experienced a problem and responded to it by creating an innovative solution. Sara Blakely founded Spanx when she could not wear a pair of white pants without nylons, but still wanted to wear sandals. Footless pantyhose became her first product. Through sheer tenacity to make her product succeed, Sara built a net worth of over a billion dollars.

Payal Kadakia was frustrated by wasting hours trying to find a fitness class in her New York neighborhood. That frustration sparked the idea for ClassPass, which has raised over $48 million in investment funding todate and gives athletes and fitness enthusiasts access to myriad boutique gym classes across the U.S.

Jennifer Hyman and Jennifer Fleiss came up with the concept for Rent the Runway when Hyman's sister was frantically trying to find a dress to wear to a wedding. Their solution to the "nothing in my closet" drama was to create a website where women could rent designer dresses for all of the special occasions in their lives for a fraction of the cost of purchasing a single-occasion dress.

Three tedious and time-consuming trips to acquire a new driver's license under my married name sparked the idea for MissNowMrs.com, my online name change service for brides. Using technology to condense the 13-hour hassle of working through the name change process created a business that has grown over 300,000 customers and generated millions in revenue.

Evaluating Your Idea

You are no different than any entrepreneur at his or her beginning. Decide to rise. If you have a problem and see a possible solution, you too, can take the next step in the entrepreneurial process. Determine whether the problem that you are experiencing is unique to you and your situation. If that is the case, it is probably not business-worthy as there will not be a market large enough to support your idea for a product or service. However, if a significant percentage of the population encounters your problem, it is worthy of further evaluation, and it might be a business opportunity with a viable market.

Do not be afraid to talk about your idea with others. Many new entrepreneurs worry that someone they discuss their idea with might steal it.

In reality, an idea is worthless until a company that generates income is built around it. Talk to your friends and family members about your idea and listen to their feedback. The more angles and opinions you solicit, the more you will learn about your idea's strengths and weaknesses.

Now that you have an idea to evaluate, it is time to understand how it relates to innovation. Innovation is the process of bringing together old and new ideas in an original or fresh way to provide a better solution that impacts the world. Another way to look at this concept is that an idea is not an innovation unless it creates new levels of consumer satisfaction or demand.[1]

Does your idea create new levels of consumer satisfaction or demand with a truly unique service or product, or is it doing the same thing as existing companies and products in a new location (e.g., another dry cleaner but on a different corner)? While it is possible to make money creating a "me too" product, such as decorative wine glasses. If you want to be a successful entrepreneur, it is important to have a truly unique idea. Objectively look at your idea. Are you really solving a problem in a new and better way? Are you making your idea or solution more accessible to more people, thus creating more demand?

The concept of "scalability" is a critical concern. Understanding if your idea has the ability to handle the process of growth into large successful company will help you make the right decisions for you and your business. Elizabeth Kraus, Founder of MergeLane, the leading startup investment accelerator for high-growth companies with at least one female in leadership, has vast experience with entrepreneurs and startups. Her 12-week MergeLane programs match female founders that have companies between pre-revenue and $5 million with mentors and investors. Kraus's number one piece of advice: "Look at your idea from the business perspective, not the consumer perspective. Women tend to start companies that solve problems that they have experienced without looking to see if solutions already exist or what the size of the market is."

Determining the size of your potential market is essential when evaluating your idea. Small markets may seem easier to enter, but the smaller the number of customers you can sell to, the harder you will have to work to make a profit. Kraus explains, "Female founders think that if they keep things small and in control it will make their lives easier. In reality, having a non-scalable business that requires your personal time is far harder than creating a company with intellectual property that can scale."

Comparing two companies, like Garmin and Waze, is a great way to explore the concept of innovation in a real life scenario. Navigating from point A to point B has been a problem since human travel began. Getting lost, detours, construction, and accidents are just a few of the pain points involved with travel. Maps were an early solution to these problems, but more innovative solutions have been conceived and implemented as technology has progressed.

Garmin was the company who took military and aviation GPS technology and repurposed it as a product the general public could purchase to improve the way they navigated roads and highways. Their idea was innovative because it used technology in a new way and created a new consumer market for it. One drawback to Garmin devices was static maps that had to be manually updated as they became obsolete. A second limitation was a product price of several hundred dollars, which limited the driving population to the segment who could afford to purchase one. A third limitation was that a separate device was required to use Garmin's technology.

When Waze, a smartphone app, entered the navigation market, it disrupted the concept of paying for a navigational device, while also improving the existing technology by adding real-time traffic speeds fed in by live users. This allowed Waze to re-route users and save them time as it guided them on roads and highways. Without the need to manufacture a tangible navigation product, Waze was able to offer their technology free of charge, which eradicated the barrier to entry created by a purchase price. The founders of Waze ultimately sold their company to Google in 2013 for $1.3 billion.

The Garmin/Waze comparison is an example of innovation applied to ideas, where one innovation piggybacking off of an existing idea created both new levels of consumer satisfaction and new levels of consumer demand.

Features and Benefits

Now that you understand the concept of innovation applied to ideas, it is time to explore the differences between features and benefits. Knowing the difference will enable you to determine if your idea creates real benefits resulting in new levels of consumer satisfaction, and how the two are used in making your product or idea salable.

A feature is a factual statement about the product or service you possess. Features are important to a product, but they alone do not entice customers to purchase the product. An example of a feature is: "our café is open 24 hours."

A benefit is an explanation of "what's in it for me" for the consumer. A benefit is the positive result of a feature. An example of a benefit of "our café is open 24 hours" is that a customer can eat or caffeinate whenever they want.

If you try to sell a product using only its features, the potential customers have to figure out how the feature results in a benefit to them. Painting a picture of how a feature benefits your target customer simplifies the sale. To continue with the example: "Our café is open 24 hours so you can buy a cappuccino at 2:00 a.m. when you are cramming for a final."

Consumers don't care about features, they care about benefits. Make sure that your idea or product features create true benefits for your target market. Without benefits, your idea is not an innovation and you may need to go back to the drawing board. Unless real users can identify, as well as desire, the benefits of your product feature, you don't have a salable product.

As you uncover and understand the benefits of your product or idea, it is time to look at your idea and decide if you have a new product or a new feature for an existing product. A product is an item or solution that is manufactured or refined for sale. Products are what you sell to create revenue. A tube of lipstick is a product. A feature is a distinctive characteristic or element of something. The use of natural ingredients is a feature, the benefit of that feature is the user's lips feel softer and more kissable when wearing the lipstick. You emphasize and utilize benefits to sell products.

How can you determine whether your idea is a stand-alone product worthy of building a company around, or a feature for an existing product that can be sold or licensed to another company? This question plagues all entrepreneurs, including myself, so I created the innovation gauntlet to make finding the answer easier. Use my innovation gauntlet to discover if your idea is a product or feature, and to decide if it is wise to invest your time building a company around it.

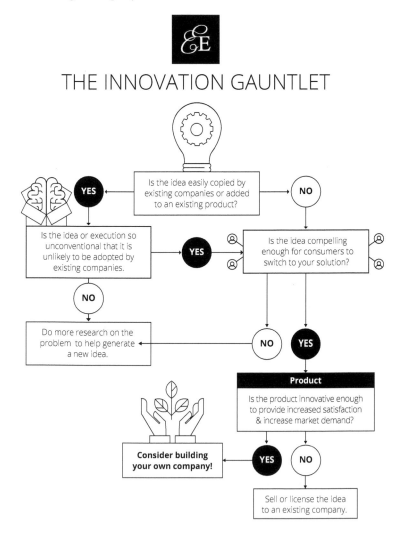

THE INNOVATION GAUNTLET

YES ← Is the idea easily copied by existing companies or added to an existing product? → **NO**

Is the idea or execution so unconventional that it is unlikely to be adopted by existing companies. → **YES** → Is the idea compelling enough for consumers to switch to your solution?

NO

Do more research on the problem to help generate a new idea. ← **NO** | **YES**

Product
Is the product innovative enough to provide increased satisfaction & increase market demand?

Consider building your own company! ← **YES** | **NO**

Sell or license the idea to an existing company.

Ask yourself and others: Is your idea easily copied by an existing company or added to an existing product. If the answer is "yes," ask yourself if your idea or its execution is unconventional and unlikely to be implemented by an existing company. If so, companies may ignore your idea because it is "simply not done." For example, car companies could have easily put a battery in their existing cars like Tesla first did with the Roadster but they 'knew' it wouldn't work. No American entrepreneur had successfully established a car company since Walter Chrysler in 1925, but the choice of car industry leaders to ignore an unconventional idea allowed Elon Musk, the CEO of Tesla, to disrupt their industry and become the premier electric vehicle manufacturer. Tesla reported over $3.1 billion in revenue in 2014, a testament to the success of unconventional ideas.

If you answered "no" to the unconventional question, your idea is most likely a feature. If the answer is "no" to the copying question or "yes" to the unconventional question ask yourself and others: Is your idea compelling enough for consumers to switch from their current solution to yours? If the answer is a resounding "yes," you have a product!

Here comes the big final question of the equation: Is your product innovative enough to warrant building a company around it? Does it truly provide increased levels of satisfaction through features and benefits to the point where it will result in increased market demand for your product?

If you answered "no" you have not failed, you simply have different avenues to consider. A product that is too small to support an entire company can be sold to a company that already has an infrastructure and is established in the market. You will receive the reward of a sale and the enjoyment of watching your product benefit customers without the risk of launching a startup.

> *Startup, business, enterprise, and company are used interchangeably throughout this book. It can be debated that there are technical differences in these terms, but for these purposes they are used to reference an ongoing organization involved in the trade of goods, services, or both, to consumers.*

Selling Your Idea

So how do you sell an idea to an existing company? It may seem daunting, but there are three channels—scaling up from big, bigger, biggest—to use when looking for a potential buyer.[2] Each requires some research on your part. If you are a willing investigator, you can search for the individuals and companies that need your product to grow and they will be happy to pay you for your idea.

Big Channel

If your idea is within a focused market or niche, make a list of the companies most likely to purchase your product or idea. Then, sift through each company's website and/or online employee directory for someone with a title including corporate development. Another easy option is to call their 800 number and ask for the corporate development head. Individuals involved in corporate development are looking for ideas and companies to acquire, making them the ideal people to pitch and sell to. Most large corporations understand the need to access and outsource innovation.

Bigger Channel

Do you have an idea that benefits large businesses in an established industry? After making a list of the best possible purchasers for your idea or product, narrow your list to companies who have corporate venture arms. These companies have already set aside company funds to invest in new products and ideas, so they are always open to pitches and purchases. How do you find out if a company you have on your prospect list has a venture investment arm? Check their company website, study their annual report and sleuth LinkedIn for contacts within the corporation. Best yet, pick up the phone and ask the front desk if there is a corporate investment arm that you can discuss your offering with. The receptionist has no idea who you are, and will be more concerned with finding the correct answer to your question than how nervous you feel exposing yourself by asking.

Biggest Channel

If you are shooting for the stars, research the roster of the Licensing Executive Society (LES) at lesusacanada.org. If a company has a LES member on staff, that person's job within the company is to license products that are not actual companies. This is also known as looking for in-licensing opportunities. LES members typically license ideas for Fortune 1000 companies, so they are big fish working for whales. It is well worth the effort to find their names on the LES site and search to see where they are employed.

Entrepreneur

If your idea made it through the innovation gauntlet, then you should consider building a company to help support and scale the sales of your product. Building a company is no simple feat. Your idea needs to be strong enough financially to support you, your cofounders, and a growing team while it competes for attention and sales in a global marketplace.

There are more questions than answers at this point, but it is important to properly frame, ask, and find the answers to the following questions: Is the growth potential there for you to make enough money to get through that initial phase? How strong are the existing competitors in the industry? Have you built a company before? Are you prepared to assemble a team of individuals who can support and grow your product? Answering these questions will help you address the idea of building a company with your eyes wide open.

If building a company sounds overwhelming, you have other options to consider. Just because you generated an innovative idea does not mean that you must be the person to build it into a company. Think about what would make you happy and what is best for the growth of your idea. You can enjoy the satisfaction of selling or licensing your idea to another company, without the risk of building a company yourself.

For example, do you love yoga and have an innovative idea for a yoga studio? Do you want to grow your idea into a yoga studio in every major city in your state or even nationally? Decide whether putting all of your time and effort into growing a company that supports your studios will make you happy. As you launch your company, your time will be taken by pressing business matters like funding, employee training, advertising, and growth. You will have very little time to spend practicing or teaching yoga. Do you just want to practice yoga where you want, when you want? The answers to these questions will help you decide if entrepreneurship is right for you.[3]

Excited to build a company around your innovative idea? Good for you! You had the idea, you passed it through the innovation gauntlet, examined its features and benefits, weighed its salability, and decided whether it was large enough to build a company around. It has emerged triumphant. This is it! You have the vision of all the steps that will lead to your success. This fully realized vision and understanding will fuel your passion for your idea and, in time, your success.

Do not be dissuaded by those who cannot see the dots to your success. You are privileged to see the world in a different way than most. This is an asset and should be cherished, even if in the short term you are the only one who cherishes it. As long as the fundamentals of what makes an innovation are met, you are responsible for believing in yourself and your idea. You have to be your biggest promoter and idea evangelist.

Chapter 1 Takeaways

- Don't waste time solving a problem that very few people encounter, even if your solution is elegant.
- An idea is not an innovation unless it creates new levels of satisfaction or demand.
- Having an innovative idea doesn't always mean that you should build a company to support it.
- Inventors can create unique products that allow established companies to manufacture and market said products.

How It Feels

Having a big idea feels exciting and a little dangerous. What you choose to do with your idea has the impetus to change your entire life. You can be filled with euphoria and feel like a genius one moment, then wonder if you are delusional the next.

Putting your big idea through the innovation gauntlet is tough. It is possibly the first time you are applying business methodology to question your idea's long-term success. This is a scary concept, especially if you are counting on your big idea to get you out of your current job or life situation.

Further Reading

The Myths of Innovation by Scott Berkun
The E-Myth Revisited by Michael E. Gerber

[1.] Concept voiced by Peter Drucker in *Innovation and Entrepreneurship*

[2.] Concept shared by Andrew J. Sherman

[3.] Concept voiced by Michael E. Gerber in *E-Myth Revisited*

ANSWERS ARE FREE,

MISTAKES ARE COSTLY.

~ DANIELLE TATE ~

*Elegant*ENTREPRENEUR

ASK THE RIGHT QUESTIONS
OF THE RIGHT PEOPLE

Everyone likes to feel completely confident and knowledgeable in matters pertaining to their startup or business. Our society places tremendous importance on "having your act together" and "having all the answers." Buying into that facade can hurt you and your business much more than it can help you.

In reality, launching a business involves more questions than answers. No matter how many years of experience you have in business, marketing, or a particular industry, that time investment does not give you all the answers needed to create a successful enterprise. Being afraid to ask the hard questions will cripple you and inhibit your company's growth.

Entrepreneurs who ask for help and wisdom when faced with challenges are exponentially more successful than their peers who cobble together solutions to save face. The Startup Genome Report Extra on Premature Scaling[4], a project coauthored by University of California, Berkeley and Stanford faculty members with Steve Blank, makes such a conclusion. The project found that startups that have helpful mentors, effectively track metrics, and learn from startup thought leaders raise 7 times more money and have 3.5 times better user growth. Tapping into the wealth of other entrepreneurs can be as formal as creating an advisory board for your startup, or as informal as meeting for coffee with someone knowledgeable in your idea area.

Whatever your meeting format, be prepared with a list of the most important questions you need answered to develop your idea. Don't be afraid to ask the scary questions such as "Is there really a market for my idea?"; "Is my solution executable on a large scale?"; "Does the technology exist to support my idea?"; and "How do I manufacture my product?". Formulating and asking specific, detailed questions is essential to uncovering the exact data or wisdom you need.

Poor Question Example: *Do you know someone who builds websites?*

Specific Question Example: *How would you locate and select a PHP programmer who is looking to join a startup?*

Equally important is directly asking the people best suited to answering your question. Experts and founders in any industry love to give advice to people who are smart enough to ask an intelligent question, and who actually listen to and implement their answers/suggestions. It may be difficult to get through the various gatekeepers shrouding your ideal source of wisdom, but when you reach them there will be a huge payout of answers.

The web is the ultimate tool to use when tracking down your ideal source. Search the Internet for experts in the field of your question, or industry leaders that have the answers you need. Make a "punch list" of possible sources. Prioritize your punch list and start sleuthing. If you have any personal connections, no matter how minute, ask for an introduction. If you aren't connected to your ideal expert, Google the top person's name and look for their email address, phone number, or Twitter handle. Many times their corporate site will not list this information, but an interview or blog post might. Next, plug their name into the search box of LinkedIn and look for a contact you have in common who could facilitate an introduction. If you do not have a shared contact you can inbox message the person.

While it is important to look for a personal introduction to an expert, it is not necessary to have one to contact them. If you truly need to speak to someone you are not connected with, pick up the phone and call them. An example of a cold call yielding great results is the story of how the founders of LegalZoom convinced Robert Shapiro to join their company. Legal-

ASK THE RIGHT QUESTIONS

Zoom began offering legal service products to the masses in 2001, but the founders realized that they needed a high profile lawyer as a partner to gain the public's trust. They decided Robert Shapiro, most recognized for successfully defending O. J. Simpson in 1995, was the ideal candidate, but since none of them knew him personally, they sourced his phone number and called him. The results of that 8:30 p.m. call was a direct connection with Robert, who agreed to become a cofounder to support LegalZoom.

Twitter is the backdoor to big names in business. I have had remarkable success tweeting to access individuals I want to connect with. Just be sure to tweet something that will catch their attention and pique their interest enough to respond to you. For example, after numerous failed attempts to make contact with a potential partner I sent the following tweet to the company's president:

@chrisjbraun message our CEO about a partnership with NameChangeNextStep, MissNowMrs & GetYourNameBack #goodidea

My tweet resulted in an immediate response and partnership phone call with NOLO, a large legal services company I had been trying to connect with for months.

Another Twitter tip is to add a professional photo of your product or yourself in your tweet to catch your contact's attention and boost your credibility.

Mentors

Ingrid Vanderveldt, the founder and CEO of EBW2020, offers her number one piece of advice for new entrepreneurs "Get yourself a mentor!" EBW2020 is a virtual accelerator with the goal of empowering one billion women to succeed as leaders and entrepreneurs by 2020. Vanderveldt's numerous companies and entrepreneurial experience led her to create this platform which provides women with online tools, education, mentors, and business support, thus changing the world for female founders.

Entrepreneurs of all industries emphasize the value of a mentor. But if you are new to the entrepreneurial world, where do you look for a mentor? EBW2020 has a free mentor-matching platform to connect fledgling founders with experts in their fields. Looking for a more direct approach to finding a mentor? Almost every city or community has an accelerator. An accelerator is a company or group that takes a small amount of equity in return for small amounts of capital and mentorship through a multi-month program. Internet research will locate ones near you. Another option is to attend meetups devoted to your area of interest and meet like-minded mentors there. If you are unfamiliar with meetups, they are in-person meetings created to bring communities together. Interests range from dog breed enthusiasts to photography buffs, to female founders within a specific city. There are thousands of meetups in any city, simply identify and attend the ones that are aligned with your needs and interests.

Identifying your ideal mentor based on their previous companies, field of expertise, and connection to your industry is easy. Persuading industry moguls to become your mentor is a challenge. Vanderveldt suggests finding ways to help your potential mentor achieve their goals and then offering them your assistance. "This will place you in their sphere and will allow natural conversations about what you are working on to occur." These conversations can lead to long-term relationships and mentorship.

Caren Merrick is a serial entrepreneur who cofounded software company webMethods. She shares that the most influential mentor she had "is the former president of a $1 billion recruitment company; she also serves on public company boards where only 17-18% are women." Merrick's relationship with her mentor grew as her company grew—webMethods is now a global public company of $200 million and 1,100 employees. Now, as the current Founder and CEO of Pocket Mentor, Merrick's joy is inspiring leaders to discover and achieve their potential. She says, "my mentor continues to encourage me to think bigger, say 'no' to some opportunities, and challenge my self-limiting beliefs (which strike all of us regardless of how many goals and successes we have achieved). I have been delighted to help her, too, for example, when I learned that a company was looking for a board member, I suggested her, and I have introduced her to a few women in my network that would be mutually beneficial for them and her." This is a prime example of an entrepreneur finding an ideal mentor and developing a relationship of mutual support.

Be diligent in your searching and bold in your asking. The harder you try, the more likely you will uncover the needed information. Be sure to ask the correct question of the correct person. Their answers are key to you building a successful startup, so it is worth the effort.

Meredith Fineman, founder of FinePoint, shares her theory on mentors: "The concept of mentorship is shifting. No one person is going to fulfill your every need. Create a collective brain trust of individuals in many industries, not just yours." Mentors in all stages of life and a variety of industries can provide you with perspective you could miss if you focus on finding one person within your industry to listen to. Be open to wisdom from anyone.

Once you have access to your ideal answer contact or contacts, take the time to research their professional background via Google, LinkedIn and Wikipedia. Be respectful, attentive, and accept the suggestions provided by your contact—this is critical to acquiring valuable advice. No one enjoys investing their time offering strategies and guidance to someone who is unyielding, unresponsive, and doesn't intend to apply such offerings.

Ask your all-important question and then shut up, actively listen, and take notes. Ruminate on ideas that seem "out there" for a few days before discarding them, and always mail a thank you note to the person who shared their wisdom. A grateful spirit is noticed and admired in any industry.

If you want to see your startup succeed, you'll need to prioritize its needs above your personal pride. That does not imply that you have to wring your hands and beg for assistance when you have questions. Intelligent entrepreneurs appreciate someone who can ask for help instead of hiding behind ego, and typically will go out of their way to aid them. Request help in a professional manner and you will receive it. If for some reason your first source turns you down, simply ask the next best person on your "punch list" (that's why you made it). No one expects you to build a startup in a vacuum.

Elegant Insight 1 Takeaways

- Not asking questions is fatal for your startup.
- Formulate the right questions and ask the best possible source for the answer.
- The Internet has made tracking down and accessing your ideal source easy.
- Ask advisors, mentors, and experts to answer your burning business questions.

How It Feels

Generating a huge list of questions about your startup and field can make you feel queasy and clueless. Do not overwhelm yourself by trying to answer all of the questions simultaneously (you will never get anywhere). You can use the framework of this book to prioritize what obstacle is impeding your progress today, and focus on finding that specific answer. For example, in determining if your idea meets the criteria of "innovative," focus your questions around how the problem is specifically defined and exactly how your solution meets those needs for consumers.

Asking for help can make you feel incompetent and exposed, especially if you open up to the wrong person about your problem. If you approach the wrong person, do not be discouraged and do not give up. Discovering the wrong person should give you additional insight into who the right person should be. Refocus your energy on finding the right person with the knowledge and ability to solve your problem. Asking a qualified person for help and wisdom will almost always help you feel more positive about finding a solution. The more positivity you have going for your startup, the better. So do a little research for a mentor, find the right person for your particular question and ask away!

---

4. Startup Genome Report Extra on Premature Scaling: https://s3.amazonaws.com/startupcompass-public/StartupGenomeReport2_Why_Startups_Fail_v2.pdf

YOUR LARGEST FEAR
CARRIES YOUR
GREATEST GROWTH.

*Elegant*ENTREPRENEUR

VALIDATION & MARKET RESEARCH

Validating and researching your idea or product is one of the most important steps in the journey to entrepreneurial success. It is easily rushed through or skipped over in the excitement of wanting to launch a business as soon as possible. Who wants to spend time sending surveys and crunching data when you can be spending time on fun things like designing your logo, website, and business cards? No one, but research is paramount to the success of your company. Resist the allure of all of the imaginative details that want to claim your attention. Focus your energy on research instead.

Donna Harris, Cofounder of 1776, a global incubator that finds and funds the best ideas and people, advises entrepreneurs to view their startup as if they're building a house. "There is a reason you build a foundation before a roof. Get your problem-to-solution fit right to create a firm foundation to build your company on. Some business decisions are directly related to its foundation—if you make a mistake your company will fail. Other decisions are comparable to paint colors—if you make a mistake you repaint."

Research will reveal if your idea or product is a good one, if there are people who want it enough to purchase it, how many potential customers there are, and how much they're willing to pay. You need these answers before you can begin to decide if your idea is worth your full commitment and capital. Marsha Firestone, president and founder of the Women Presidents' Organization, believes it is essential for entrepreneurs to validate their market. Firestone emphasizes, "Be sure that there is an interest and a need for your product or service. Do your market research."

Undertaking market research seems to fill aspiring entrepreneurs with dread. Why? Many women fear the results of their research could nip their idea in the veritable bud. In reality, the more you know about your market and how your idea or product does or does not fit into it is the key to building a successful company. The reward in understanding what consumers in your target market truly want can help you pivot, or abruptly change, your idea to something that will instantly work. Inadequate research could result in launching a company that tanks in the first six months. Going into business with your eyes wide open will save you time, money, and tears.

Your time and money are incredibly valuable—you cannot afford to waste them by investing them in building a product or service that fails. The more you test your product or service before you build and sell it, the more likely you are to earn the profit that you desire. Harris explains the importance of testing: "Figure out what is fact and what is assumption when talking about your startup. Find out what is true by running tests. Order your testing large to medium, because the little stuff doesn't matter in the beginning." Her honest observation is, "Many entrepreneurs fail because they mistake an assumption about a vital part of their business as a fact." Heed Harris's advice and commit to market research and testing.

JetBlue is a stellar example of a company using market research to understand consumer needs before building their product. JetBlue's market analysis found that airline passengers cared more about comfortable leather seats and in-flight entertainment than a hot meal, a first class cabin, or other amenities offered by established airlines. Using this data, JetBlue invested in upgraded seating, satellite radio, and TVs, while emphasizing a relaxing flight at a relatively modest price. JetBlue's launch filled a consumer need and allowed them to successfully enter the competitive commercial airline market and become the fifth largest airline in the United States.

Another reason entrepreneurs often put market research on the backburner, is that the task can seem overwhelming or borderline impossible. Often first-time founders don't know where to begin in the process. What questions do you ask? How do you find the right consumers to answer the questions? How do you analyze the results of your research? Keil Oliver, a former acquisition manager for the U.S. Department of Defense shares: "As a civil servant, market research was part of our acquisition plan. Often we skipped that step because it was too daunting. The downfall was that the skipping for us resulted in stifled innovation. We ultimately went the easy route with the big companies who charged an arm and a leg instead of finding out if there was a capable small business." As is the case with most daunting tasks, breaking the market research process into individual steps will help make it more manageable.

Market Research and Customer Development

The first step is formulating questions. Is your idea or product the result of a problem or pain that you faced? How painful and frequent is the frustrating problem you encountered? Is it something that you would pay any amount of money to never repeat, or is it something that is annoying but livable? The answers to these questions play into how much you will be able to charge for your solution. How much you can charge, and in turn, profit from supplying your solution are key factors in whether you should continue exploring and researching your business idea.

Next, identify consumers in your target market. Is a specific segment of the population experiencing the problem you are solving? Children, brides, teachers, retirees, and veterans are examples of such segments. As you identify the segment or segments that experience your same problem, be mindful of how easy they are to locate and market to. If your problem is part of a life stage inflection point such as college graduation, death, marriage, retirement or motherhood, it will be easier to find potential customers and market your solution to them.

Dedicate time to understanding exactly who your potential customers are and what makes them tick. Determine their age range, where they live, where they work, what careers they typically have, as well as their median income. Complete ethnographic research to understand the culture of your potential customers. What do they like to do? Where do they look for solutions to their problems (Google, Pinterest, word of mouth, celebrities)? The answers to these questions will help you locate and access your potential customers.

Leslie Bradshaw is the former COO, president and cofounder of JESS3, a creative agency specializing in social media marketing, branding, web design, and data visualization. Bradshaw grew her company by 4000% from 2007 to 2011. She stresses the importance of research, "Don't underestimate desk research. You can unearth volumes via Google Scholar (a free search engine for scholarly articles, theses, books, abstracts, and court opinions, from academic publishers, professional societies, universities, and web sites) and talking to people notable in the industry you are considering to enter. A talk with the right person can reveal companies who failed to solve the problem previously, companies working on a solution similar to yours and insights into the market needs."

Now go sit down with real, live strangers who represent your potential customers. You can go to where your customers are and bring your product, do an online survey, or even offer to purchase coffee for strangers in a Starbucks in exchange for their feedback. Ask specific questions about the problem you are solving, and request feedback about both pros and cons. What issues does the problem cause for the customer? Then ask each customer how your solution relates to their problem and how much they would pay for it. This can be as simple as asking people directly for their opinions and writing down their answers. Or you may create a question on Facebook and have your friends answer it and share it with their friends.

Example: If you have a new product that tracks dehydration in runners, attend a marathon and ask 50 participants if they would pay $20 for your product. If not, why not? What are they looking for in the solution and what would they be willing to pay?

What do you do if you do not have access to people who experience your problem? There is a company called AYTM (Ask Your Target Market) that lets you survey your target market out of their 25 million respondents using their survey and reporting tools. It is a fast and inexpensive way to start learning about your potential customers.

The more data you can collect, the more accurate assumptions can be gleaned. Surveys are a great way to collect mass data for minimal investment. Products like Google Forms or SurveyMonkey allow you to create a multi-question survey in minutes and email it to any list you have. Keep your survey concise and try not to lead respondents with your questions. Consumer answers from a personal viewpoint are always the most interesting and insightful. Providing space for a free-form typed answer for each multiple choice option will allow people to express exactly what they think and want, even if you missed it with your answer choices.

Once you have amassed customer feedback, analyze it to understand the exact pain or challenge your target customers are experiencing, the solution they want, and a price they are willing to pay. Now compare their ideal solution with your idea. Ideally the two will overlap. If they don't, you will need to adjust your product or service to better align with your market needs. The bottom line: customers only buy what they perceive as the perfect solution, not what you perceive as the perfect solution.

Once you have honed in on the best possible version of your idea, consider designing a crowdfunding campaign on a website like KickStarter or Indiegogo. This type of campaign is a fantastic way to market your product 3-4 months prior to launch, and to build a community of early supporters. When strategically planned and implemented as a serious marketing tool, these platforms enable your current network, as well as strangers, to pledge money to fund your project after learning more about it. If thousands of people love your idea enough to give you money, you can feel confident in both your idea and of a viable market.

The Pebble wristband is an excellent example of successful crowdfunding for a new product. It works with iPhone and Android apps to give users instant, easy notifications of important calls, emails, or other app alerts via the display on its digital face. Within 28 hours of posting a Kickstarter campaign, Pebble received $1 million and went on to raise more than $10 million in funding for their project.

If your crowdfunding campaign does not meet its goals, you need to pinpoint why. Examine your messaging and pricing, as well as the features and benefits of your product. Ask potential backers what they do not understand and/or do not like about your sales proposition. Use their answers to revamp and launch a new campaign. Take the perspective that you are learning exactly what your customer wants for free instead of you spending your time and money developing something they won't buy.

The amount of information you gather from consumer opinions is nothing less than staggering. People love to voice their opinions and have them matter. Take these veritable gems and treat them as such. Categorize your findings and use them to fine tune your solution and how you present and price it.

Competitive Review

Analyzing your competition is one of the most important first steps toward determining whether your product or service will be a success or not. If the marketplace is saturated with similar ideas, you will quickly realize your product or service suffers from a weak business model. By investigating the marketplace, creating comprehensive market analysis, and devising effective strategies upfront, you will improve your chances of having a competitive edge, while also uncovering the strengths and weaknesses of your market segment. Be clever and creative with your competitive review. Consider everything: from geographic area to indirect competitors; who your top five competitors are; your ability to compete, what makes you more valuable to the marketplace than your competitors. Take these steps and create your own competitive review:

STEP 1. Scour the Internet and make an exhaustive list of any company who could be considered remotely competitive with your idea or who is attempting to solve the same problem. It's very easy to skim over competitors and mentally say "I'm not like them" or "Mine is better than that." Researching every potential competitor's strengths and weaknesses can help you better understand how to differentiate your product or service.

STEP 2. Objectively study and document their products, websites, company literature, social media accounts, and press. Journalize your research to be thorough. It will force you to articulate the difference between your product offering and your competitors' and it will capture the information so you can refer back over time.

STEP 3. Ask Competitive Review Questions:

What do you like about their branding and messaging?

What are their best features?

What do consumers like best about their product (look at reviews)?

What do consumers like least about their product (look at reviews)?

Are they solving the problem efficiently?

How does their price compare to the entire competitive market and your prices?

Will customers be willing to pay you more for your solution?

The answers to these questions will help you position your company and hone the way you represent your brand. It will also help you avoid any mistakes that your competitor has made, enhancing your business from the beginning.

STEP 4. Now it is time to analyze where your competition sources their online customers. Invest in comparison software, such as Market Samurai or SEM Rush, to scrutinize the volume of visitors coming to their website. Check which keywords show up organically, which keywords they pay to advertise on, and which websites link to them. Do not be concerned about using tools to understand your competition. Competitive information is gold when you are starting a company and rest assured your competitors will be analyzing your company as soon as they know about it. Business is business, it's not personal.

Keywords are the words or phrases that potential customers type into a search engine when they are looking for information, a product or solution. Be sure to use those specific keyword phrases as much as possible on your website and blog without diluting your message.

Exploring which websites and companies have links to your competitors will provide a list of potential resellers, influencers, and partners to acquire or have link to your website. The best strategic partnerships in business happen when neither company is afraid of losing something to the other, and both benefit each other or each other's customers.

Chapter 2 Takeaways

- Don't skip or skimp on validating your idea and market.
- Use surveys and the feedback to understand the solution your customers want.
- Learn from your competition.

How It Feels

Asking consumer opinions on your solution or product is uncomfortable because there is the possibility of negative feedback. As women, we shy away from anything that might cause discomfort, especially about things close to the heart. It's like asking a group of friends if your significant other is "marriage material." No one wants to hear anything but rave reviews . . . but reality will catch up with you regardless. Better to know the truth upfront so you can make decisions to improve your idea or move on to others.

Further Reading

The Lean Startup by Eric Ries

Lean Customer Development: Building Products Your Customers Will Buy by Cindy Alvarez

Just Enough Research by Erika Hall

Get Funded: A Kick-ass Plan for Running a Successful Crowdfunding Campaign by Nicole Delger

Hacking Kickstarter, Indiegogo: How to Raise Big Bucks in 30 Days: Secrets to Running a Successful Crowd Funding Campaign on a Budget by Patrice Williams Marks

I DON'T HAVE DREAMS

I HAVE PLANS.

~ RACHEL WOOD ~

*Elegant*ENTREPRENEUR

DON'T FALL IN LOVE BEFORE HOLDING YOUR IDEA ACCOUNTABLE

Would you marry someone and throw all of your financial and emotional resources into this individual without knowing if they were a good person or what their life ambitions were? Hopefully the answer to that question is "no." Much like the beginning of a romantic relationship, it is in your best interest to fully know your startup idea's best points and worst points. Identify areas that need work and assess the realistic scope of your startup's potential success before you devote yourself to it. No amount of love and energy can change a bad idea into a good one, so don't waste your valuable time and startup zeal on something that will never make it off the ground.

It's very easy to get caught up thinking about all of the money your idea is going to make and how famous you are going to be. The mansion you're going to live in, the yacht that you'll vacation on, and how your idea is going to positively impact the world are all fabulous things to dream about. Sadly, the more you embellish daydreams about your idea, the harder it is going to be for you to admit if your idea turns out to be unfeasible or just not that great. Your idea is worthless unless you can build a product, execute a profitable business model, and sustain a company around it, so don't get too attached to ideas.

Ingrid Vanderveldt, of EBW2020, experienced this dilemma with her first company 212 Studios, an online data mining and analysis company.

She reflects, "The company was a disaster. I was so in love with what we were attempting to do—save the world—that it was hard to be objective about growth." Vanderveldt raised $7 million in investment capital for 212 Studios, but eventually sold the company assets during the dot com bust. Her advice: "You create a business because you see an opportunity or you are passionate about solving a problem. Parking lot that emotion and focus on putting your business together piece by piece, looking through the lens of money. You need money to succeed."

Separate "you" from "your idea." Evaluating "your idea" is personal and can make you blind to issues, as well as defensive about constructive criticism. Evaluating "an idea" allows you to make lists of pros and cons without clouded judgement or embarrassment if it turns out to be mediocre. You can easily rebound with the next round of ideas when you're not in love with "your idea."

Now is the time to become an expert on your problem and idea. If there are any journal articles or books on the problem or similar solutions, read them all. Glean any facts and statistics that you find pertinent. Then try them out on your test audience. Confirm that academia is on the money about your issue, or debunk it. When you interview, survey or solicit the opinion of the masses, the sum total is a common wisdom about your problem. True facts will guide you in building your idea into a business.

A negative response is not easily welcomed after investing time and planning into your startup. The inception point of your idea, however, is the exact time that you need to be objective. Solicit everyone and their mom's opinion on your idea. Be flexible, try to quell your objections, and record their feedback. Devote a Google document, notebook, or Evernote account to initial feedback on your idea. All opinions, both positive and negative, will be useful as you move forward.

Upon collecting opinions and feedback on your idea, sort them into positive and negative categories. As you analyze the positive and negative feedback, specifically look for comments that converge or overlap. The more feedback is repeated, the more attention you should pay to it. If you can edit your idea to overcome the problem or problems revealed via feedback, you should move forward. If you are unable to fix your idea, it might be time to let it go.

Knowledge is power. Knowledge before making a large decision is even more powerful. Take time to understand the viability of your idea before you invest yourself. A short-lived idea scrapped, then followed by an outstanding idea and startup is much better than a mediocre startup built around a shaky premise. The wisdom of the masses is just that. Use it to your benefit or ignore it to your detriment.

Elegant Insight 2 Takeaways

- Separate "you" from "your idea" to make critical evaluation easier.
- Become an expert on your problem and solution.
- If you are unable to fix your idea to overcome negative feedback, it is time to let it go.

How It Feels

Floating upward emotionally on the dream bubble surrounding a new idea is glorious. You feel smart and particularly special for having come up with such an amazing idea. Your first instinct will be to protect your "bubble" from anything that might pop it. However, becoming attached to your dream bubble is a recipe for a nightmarish fall when it pops. Take the quick pain of a new idea missing the mark over the long slow torture of watching a company you've worked to build die before it gets to market.

SHE TURNED HER
CAN'T INTO CANS AND
DREAMS INTO PLANS.

*Elegant*ENTREPRENEUR

~ Chapter 3 ~

BUSINESS PLANNING

"Plans are nothing, planning is everything," said Dwight Eisenhower, a famous quote that is particularly relevant when considering turning an idea into a business.

Planning is invaluable, even in the ever-changing world around you. As your idea changes and evolves, the exercise of mapping and recording your steps to launch a successful business is important. You will reap the benefits of understanding your market, your mission, your competitors, and how to get to your end goal. You will also identify problems and will know the solutions well before questions are raised in the competitive marketplace.

There are three main models for planning your business's success: a pitch deck, the business model canvas, or a traditional business plan. Each model has merit, and as every startup is different, you should select the model that best suits your current needs. I see any business planning model as a cross between a map, an infomercial, and a Magic 8 Ball. In each one you will need to explain your product, the problem it solves, and then forecast the success of your business.

Your business will most likely change and as it does, so too should your business plan. It is helpful to maintain older versions for reference, but if you try to run your business from older plan versions you run the risk of ending up like Blockbuster Video. Blockbuster declined a partnership pitch from industry newcomer Netflix in 2000. The result of the company's lack of foresight and inability to adapt to shifts in consumers' preferences resulted in the bankruptcy of Blockbuster in 2010, and the growth of Netflix into a $2.8 billion company (10 times Blockbuster's worth).

Be dead serious when you are creating your pitch deck, canvas, or business plan. This is the platform or presentation that can make or break your idea. Assume the audience listening to your pitch or reading your plan has zero understanding of your industry or product. Think of the questions they would have and what would confuse them. Answer those questions clearly in your planning. As you make your presentation, be diligent about including all accumulated information, which will take them from scratching their heads to opening their wallets.

Pitch Deck

A pitch deck is the most informal business planning option and can be created in PowerPoint, Keynote, Prezi, or Google slides. It is a 10-slide presentation that gives a brief and informative overview of your startup. The key to creating an effective pitch deck is using clear, concise information to tell your startup story with visual impact. It is helpful to use Guy Kawasaki's 10/20/30 rule: decks should be limited to 10 slides, present for no longer than 20 minutes, and use 30 point font or larger on your slides. Looking for inspiration? Check out pitchenvy.com or slideshare.net/500startups to browse the pitch decks of top startups.

Pitch Deck Components[5]

1. **What Your Company Does**
2. **Problem:** Help them understand and feel the pain
3. **Solution:** How your product/service solves the problem
4. **Market:** Show your market size (use a credible source so you can back it up)
5. **Business Model:** How you make money from your customers
6. **Competition:** Who your competitors are, and why you are better and different

7. **Marketing Strategy:** Where do you find your customers, and what is your cost to acquire each customer

8. **Team:** Why your team is trustworthy, awesome, and committed to the company

9. **Traction:** Monthly revenue, company growth, number of customers/ users (i.e., key performance indicators, or KPIs)

10. **Needs:** What do you need to continue to grow your startup or accelerate its growth

The pros of creating a pitch deck is that it's an easy, quick model to create, which reveals your business personality with color and graphics. This model also allows you to impart a great deal of information very quickly. Finally, a pitch deck will enable you to participate in various opportunities to receive feedback on your idea from experts and other entrepreneurs.

The big con of creating pitch deck as a planning model is its brevity. It is an overview, so you don't have space to dig into the details of how you are going to execute your idea or overcome issues. The devil is always in the details, especially in business. If a pitch deck is your only business planning tool, be sure to base your traction slide on a detailed financial model you have created in Excel.

Business Canvas

Most business model canvases are a one-page chart with nine separate sections to complete. The original business model canvas was designed by Alexander Osterwalder in 2008 to develop generic business models. New canvases for entrepreneurs, such as the Lean Canvas have been created since then to meet our niche needs.

Business Model Canvas Sections[6]

1. **Customer Segments:** Who are your potential customers
2. **Value Propositions:** The value you deliver to your customers (there can be more than one)
3. **Channels:** How your value propositions are communicated and sold to your customers

4. **Customer Relationships:** How you interact with the customer through the sale and use of your product or service
5. **Revenue Streams:** How your business makes money from your value proposition(s)
6. **Key Activities:** The strategic things your company does to deliver its value proposition
7. **Key Resources:** What your business needs to beat its competition
8. **Key Partnerships:** Outline partner participation outside your business, which frees you to focus on your business's most important projects
9. **Cost Structure:** How your decision to price and promote your product will affect your fixed and variable costs

If you have cofounders, it is advisable to print out the canvas and answer the questions together. This sets up a collaboration mode on ideas, instead of creating competing ones. Once you have completed the paper canvas to your satisfaction, download a free template to use for sharing the information digitally or for presentations.

The pros of using a business model canvas is that it is concise and information is visible on one page. This makes it easier to understand your vision and focus on what makes your business work. This format also makes it easier to test new angles, clearly identifying all segments the proposed change will impact on one page. It is a very collaborative-friendly model. If a team is involved, you can all work together instead of dividing it into individual sections to complete.

The cons to using a business model canvas is that its "simple format" is deceptively complicated and uses its own precise terminology. It also does not take into account your company's mission or your competition. If you haven't read Eric Ries's *Lean Startup*, you should, because any investment of time understanding Lean Canvas word definitions and how they interact with each other (i.e., a steep learning curve), is time well spent.

Business Plan

A business plan is a larger document that explains your business, and how each partner contributes to the business. It includes the steps necessary to go from idea to product or service, the size of the market for your business, and why your business will be successful.

Business Plan Components[7]

1. **Executive Summary:** What your company is and why your idea will be successful
2. **Description of Business:** Explanation of your company and what it does, and why it's better than any competitors (think infomercial)
3. **Market Analysis:** Assessment of the size and value of your market, customer spending and competition
4. **Organization and Management:** Who does what, who owns what, and the skills they have to make them successful
5. **Marketing and Sales:** Your marketing/sales strategy for reaching customers and selling your product
6. **Financial Projections:** How much money you will spend vs. how much you will make over time

Business plans are the most time-consuming and detailed model to execute. However, completing one is advisable and there are circumstances where it is absolutely necessary to create one. If you are incredibly anxious, creating a 25-page plan to attain success can give you a sense of peace. Likewise, if you have a cofounder you do not know well, a business plan maps out what each of the partners will do to grow the company. This becomes especially valuable in preventing the "passing of the buck" if your company isn't performing well.

If you need a business loan, lease, or access to commercial real estate, a business plan is typically a must. Personally, I was unable to meet with a commercial realtor until I was able to provide him with a complete business plan. Creating a plan shows that you have invested both a great deal of time and thought into how you will make your company successful and that you mean "business."

Andrew J. Sherman, Professor for MBA programs at Georgetown University and the University of Maryland and a Senior Partner at Jones Day, one of the world's largest law firms wrote *Start Fast Start Right* a book on business plans. He states, "business plans force entrepreneurs to have the discipline to examine the elements that are easy to skip in the other planning platforms, which are the elements that are typically fatal to a business." Sherman also advises entrepreneurs to begin by building a business canvas and use it as a bridge to take information into their pitch deck and business plan. "Business canvases make you create a business model, which both other planning platforms expand upon." Depending on your service or product, it may be prudent to invest time in creating all three business models. By looking at your company through multiple lenses you overcome the shortfalls of each model and reap all of the insights and benefits that they offer.

Chapter 3 Takeaways

- Assume the person reading your plan has zero understanding of your idea or startup and answer all of their questions.
- Be honest, enthusiastic, and concise when using a business planning model.
- Every business model has pros and cons, so pick the one that best suits your needs (or complete all of them).
- If your business planning isn't plausible, your idea probably isn't either.

How It Feels

Developing a business planning model to map your steps to success shines the stark light of reality onto your precious idea. You may cringe when you realize how many steps must occur before the launching of your product or website. It can also burst the bubble of how much revenue you can potentially earn, and highlight what pieces of planning are missing for you to be successful.

Take a moment to focus on how you feel post-business planning. Do you feel nervous but hopeful? Press on. You have written down a step-by-step plan to make your idea successful and profitable. Follow those steps faithfully and you will be justly rewarded. It won't always be easy, but it will be so worth it in the end!

Do you have a sinking feeling in the pit of your stomach that all the steps necessary to launch your idea are beyond your scope and sound like a miserable way to spend your life? Talk to a few successful entrepreneurs about your idea and its viability. If you do not want to move forward, don't. This might be your last step. You need to have at least 90% confidence and 10% grit to make it as a successful entrepreneur. The lifestyle isn't for everyone. Forcing yourself to be an entrepreneur is a guaranteed way to commit to failure for your idea and yourself.

Further Reading

Start Fast Start Right by Andrew J. Sherman

The Art of the Start by Guy Kawasaki

The One Page Business Plan for the Creative Entrepreneur by Jim Horan

---

[5.] Pitch Deck format credit to:
www.barcinno.com/10-slides-for-a-perfect-startup-pitch-deck/

[6.] Business Model Canvas format credit to Alex Corwan,
http://www.alexandercowan.com/business-model-canvas-templates/

[7.] Business Plan component credit to Andrew J. Sherman in *Start Fast Start Right*

ALWAYS CHOOSE
ATTITUDE OVER
EXPERIENCE.

~ BARBARA CORCORAN ~

Elegant ENTREPRENEUR

USE YOUR PREVIOUS WORK EXPERIENCE TO SHAPE YOUR BUSINESS & HIRE EMPLOYEES

Very few entrepreneurs were born entrepreneurs. In reality, the majority of the most successful entrepreneurs of our time spent at least a few years working a 9-5 job before building their own ideas. The intelligent entrepreneur will take the "gold" and leave the "handcuffs" of Corporate America: glean all the specialized training and education, but discard the stifling unproductive portion.

Use your experience in the workforce when you are interviewing potential employees. Were there personality types that rubbed you the wrong way? Were they more harmful than helpful to the company? Elect to hire personalities you work well with over the prickly person with the perfect resume. When deadlines are looming, you need to be able to work together without wasting energy on conflict. Also, avoid hiring the whiner who will spend more time complaining about his or her task than actually doing it. As you learned in your previous job, the weakest member of your team affects everyone's productivity.

Apply your corporate knowledge creatively. Did you spend years learning Miller Heiman or Six Sigma? You may be sick of their various mantras and teachings, but don't throw away valuable skills when you tender your resignation. Think about your startup and what it needs to grow. Think of the strengths and weaknesses of your idea, product, and team. Then kick back and allow your wealth of previous work experience to help you come up with strategies to build bigger, better, faster. If you've hired staff members that lack your years of corporate training, take time to share your wisdom and the systems you have learned with them. Both your employees and your business will benefit from your years of experience!

If it's not working, stop doing it! One of the downfalls of big business is that a company's large size can make it difficult to employ quick changes. As a startup, you are nimble and have the ability to stop whatever isn't working immediately. If you're using a technology or method that is more time-consuming than helpful, axe it. If a partially completed product or website redesign is causing more harm than good, scrap it and think of a better solution. There's no need to save face in a board room (p.s. you don't have one!). Simply find a better tool to assist you in attaining your goals and move on.

Don't work to work. The 9-5 workday does not necessarily apply to start-ups. Many times you're working 6:00 a.m. to 11:00 p.m. When there is a lull in the insanity you don't have to sit at your desk all day. Taking time away from the office is incredibly valuable to your creativity, stamina, and mental health. You will find that when you are taking a walk or relaxing with friends or colleagues the answer to a problem you've been working on will spontaneously appear. Give your brain a break and it will reward you.

Replace conference calls with in-person meetings. If you need to work with someone on a project or check on their progress, meet with them. You will find that both sides will be much more prepared for an in-person meeting. You will accomplish your goals more succinctly than if you had a conference call. When you realize that subconsciously you place more value on face-to-face time, you will be less likely to fill your calendar with less important meetings that might sneak in as calls.

One of the most overlooked keys to success in startup land is making key contacts and then following up with them to grow your business. You don't need to invest in expensive software to stay organized. Rather, resist the urge to stack business cards on your desk after an event. Discipline yourself to type your new contacts into Excel, or HubSpot's free customer relationship management tool, along with their contact information and anything relative that you discussed. Then handle your follow-up calls, or emails, in a timely fashion. Be sure to include details from the conversation you had, as well as where you met, to help your new contact remember you and the reasons connecting is beneficial.

Whatever your working past might be, you can and should draw on your prior learning and skills to build your startup. Remember, the company in which you were formerly employed was once a small idea too. Use the things that made that company successful to fuel the success of your own idea, including hiring the most successful people from that company!

Elegant Insight 3 Takeaways

- Use your previous job training to benefit your startup.
- Don't hire people with the same personalities you disliked working with, regardless of their resume.
- If it's not working, stop doing it.

How It Feels

Exiting your previous career to begin your adventure in entrepreneurship is fraught with mixed emotions. Yes, leaving the comfort of a salary is scary! However, the escape from the confines and restrictions of the workplace, boss, and job description is incredibly exhilarating. You can use both adrenalin-charged emotions to power your decisions as you build your business.

Saying farewell to coworkers may be an emotional upheaval in leaving your job. It may seem difficult to imagine a workday without your favorite colleagues, but there is a silver lining. As a founder you have the unique opportunity to build your ideal team. Imagine how exciting it will feel to work with individuals you have hand-selected based upon their skills and personalities. Also, avoid burning bridges, because you never know who will be working for a company you may need to partner with, or even be working for you in a few years.

Confidence may be your next feeling as you draw from your past experiences to implement systems that work best for you and your team. Your time there was not a waste but a taste of which systems to upcycle from your past that will grow your company. The release of former company agendas and deadlines will allow time for creativity and growth.

SURROUND YOURSELF WITH THE
DREAMERS, AND THE DOERS, THE
BELIEVERS, AND THINKERS.
BUT MOST OF ALL SURROUND
YOURSELF WITH THOSE WHO SEE
THE GREATNESS WITHIN YOU.

*Elegant*ENTREPRENEUR

~ Chapter 4 ~

BUILDING YOUR TEAM

Some entrepreneurs want all the attention focused on themselves, and every good idea and accolade received to be their own. In reality, it is quite difficult to be a successful entrepreneur in a vacuum. Being solely responsible for all innovation, manufacturing, marketing, and support for a startup is exhausting. Ideas are best shared with a cofounder, or cofounders, and polished into product improvements or marketing initiatives.

It is a rarity for a single human being to possess all of the skills necessary to run a startup. Identify the key components your business will need to thrive, and then take a good hard look at yourself and your personal strengths and weaknesses. If you are missing a component or components, look for a partner, or partners that fill those gaps in your knowledge or skill set.

Bottom line: get a cofounder. A technical person is not usually a business development person nor vice versa. Both are essential, but rarely occur in the same human. David Cohen, CEO of TechStars accelerator, says that he looks for 5 things when evaluating a startup, "Team, team, team, market, and idea." As an investor, with a portfolio of over 175 companies, Cohen's emphasis on team cannot be overlooked.

Key Attributes of a Cofounder

Accountability

A cofounder gives you accountability. It is extremely difficult to set goals for yourself and stay on track over time. With a cofounder you know that someone else is working through their goals and expects you to be succeeding at yours. Cofounders help you stay focused on building your business.

Moral Support

Starting a company is a roller coaster of emotions and finances. You will need someone to pick you up and keep you going. Only someone as equally vested as a cofounder can truly understand what you are going through and nurture you and the company.

Expertise

A cofounder will have their own areas of expertise and skills to contribute to the company. You can draw upon and learn from the strengths that you do not possess. Important areas of expertise and skills include industry experience and contacts, sales and marketing skills, writing and content creation, graphic design, programming, engineering, accounting and finance, or funding experience.

Problem Solving

When you're in the "lows," there is usually a problem. It may be that you lost a bid, ran out of money, or are experiencing a technical failure. It is easy to get and stay mired when you are single-handedly trying to fix a problem while running a company. Two heads are always better than one at coming up with solutions to the problems and implementing them.

The ideal cofounder team includes a hacker and a hustler. The hacker is the person who handles the engineering, coding, or technical requirements for your project. The hustler is a killer salesperson who understands the vision and brings in strategic partnerships on top of acquiring customers in a rapid fashion. According to the Startup Genome Report Extra on Premature Scaling, balanced teams with one technical founder and one business founder raise 30% more money, have 2.9 times more user growth and are 19% less likely to prematurely scale than technical or business-heavy founding teams. Hopefully, you are one of the essential team archetypes. Team up with the perfect partners or team members to complement your skills and build your idea into a successful business venture.

Giving up a piece of your company in exchange for a partner or partners is a huge deal. Remember, you may be able to hire or contract for company responsibilities such as design, finance, and technical support. If engineering and coding are all you need, hire a consultant. A technical founder should understand the business need and the technological solution. He or she should possess technical vision, foresight, and a solid understanding of long-term technical management, operations, and scaling.

How to Find and Select a Cofounder

A common mistake made by fledgling entrepreneurs is to source partners and employees from their family, friends, or coworkers. While support from your inner circles is very important, it is unwise to limit your search to so few people. Instead, cast a wider net by joining a local meetup group for entrepreneurs or use an online tool to find your ideal business partner.

CoFoundersLab is the largest online community of entrepreneurs who are seeking to launch a new business. Through in-person events, in nearly 40 cities and online at CoFoundersLab.com, members take advantage of a free site. This site takes into account location, industry, skills, and personality to help entrepreneurs discover and connect with the best cofounders to launch successful companies. Shahab Kaviani, Cofounder of CoFoundersLab, believes, "While there are many factors that increase your chances of success, the single biggest factor you can control is who you choose to go into business with."

Tim Chi is a former cofounder of Blackboard, and current cofounder and CEO of WeddingWire, a global online wedding marketplace with 10 million monthly users, over 650 employees and revenue of approximately $49 million in 2014. Chi agrees with Kaviani on the importance of choosing a cofounder and adds this piece of wisdom: "It is important to look at life stage alignment with potential cofounders. If you are putting together a cofounder team, look at your families. If 2 cofounders have young children and 1 cofounder is single with unlimited time to work on the business, the single cofounder will eventually resent the fact that the other two partners leave in the evenings to spend time with their families. So much of success depends on cofounder chemistry. If that starts to degrade, it negatively affects the company."

Business partnerships are paramount to spurring the growth of an idea into a startup, and into a fully functional enterprise. As in a marriage, it is vital to take your time and choose your partner wisely. Make sure that you align on work ethics, personal integrity, priorities, and end goals for the company before inking a deal that you will live with for the rest of your lives.

It is easy to find potential partners who are infatuated with the end result of your idea and company. What you need is a partner who can focus on working together to get to your end goal(s). Each of you should complete a DiSC assessment or Gallup Entrepreneurial Profile assessment separately. These personal assessment tests will help you understand how you respond to conflict, what motivates you, your strengths, what causes you stress, your entrepreneurial style, and how you solve problems. Next, share your assessment results and discuss them. Talk about how you think and how you work and then consider if your styles are complementary or destined to be combative.

How To Find A Technical Cofounder

One of the most common questions uttered by new entrepreneurs is: "How do I find a technical cofounder?" Sourcing a technical cofounder can be incredibly difficult, especially if you only have an idea or concept. Techies get pitched constantly to build someone else's ideas into a product. They hate that most pitches are solely the idea, lacking major details such as how it should be built and who is the customer base.

To pique a potential technical partner's interest, differentiate yourself from the endless hollow pitches. Be sure to have a wireframe or other documented presentation, and the working vocabulary around the technology you need for your project. A wireframe is a simple visual guide depicting what a page of a website would look like. It shows the structure of a page, without using any graphics. It is a wireframe platform that allows you to map out your business logic using drag and drop templates for buttons, charts, images and any other website component you can think of. A website flow chart or wireframe would show the core site structure and functionality, including what pages link to where. Gliffy is an online tool that enables you to quickly turn ideas into flow charts and user interface designs. A more in-depth tool, Balsamiq is the equivalent of a digital whiteboard to create wireframes. Using Gliffy or Balsamiq is much more professional and efficient than drawing on napkins to explain your idea, especially when pitching your idea to a potential technical cofounder.

Wireframe of MissNowMrs homepage created in Balsamiq

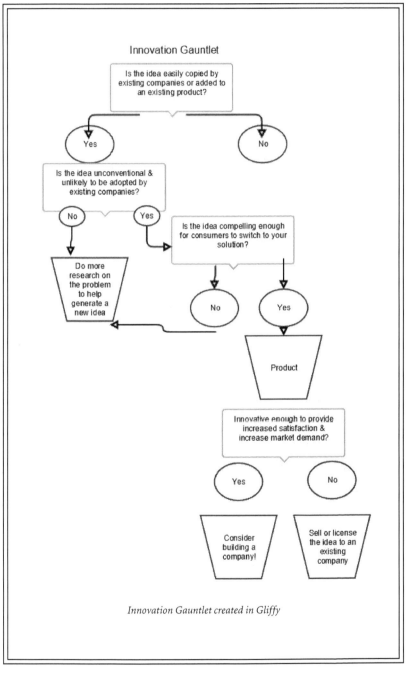

Innovation Gauntlet created in Gliffy

Sometimes the best approach is to ask for technical advice first. People love to give advice, and it can be a good way to engage technical executives well before any discussion of becoming a cofounder. If they help you work through the early steps, and you work well together, then consider discussing a cofounder partnership.

Before you use your wireframe to demonstrate your idea to potential technical partners, research the coding technology and lingo associated with building your project. Know what you need, and how to ask for it. Don't know how to spell html? Find a technical advisor to coach you on terminology and what your project requires. It is like renting a temporary Chief Technical Officer (CTO) and well worth the time investment. Finally, take time to prove the market for your idea and the viability within the market to attract customers with a new or better solution. If you can drum up large partners interested in using your solution when it is built, all the better! It is much harder to turn down a cofounder offer that is attached to an idea with a huge upside.

Armed with a wireframe, market research, and the acumen to know what technology is needed to go from idea to product, go educate and entice your potential technical cofounders. Vanessa Dawson, the founder and CEO of The Vinetta Project, advises, "Find technical cofounders in their natural habitat—attend hackathons, forums, and meetup groups specific to the technology that support your product." They will see that you are serious about your idea. They will also immediately have ideas on how to make your product better, or explain your concept more eloquently or interactively. Technical people cannot help themselves from "fixing things" so you can engage them in your idea with a simple website or wireframe, and then convert their interest into a partnership or employment opportunity.

As you evaluate potential technical cofounders, keep in mind that you do not want to give up company equity for a CPO (Chief Programming Officer), especially to someone who can simply code or develop your product. You want to exchange equity for a true CTO who can manage the building of your product, is concerned with how your solution meets customer needs, and understands the technical aspects of marketing your product such as search engine optimization and pay per click advertising. It is also important for a CTO to understand technological tradeoffs and how they affect current build goals/costs and future building goals/costs. For example, as a startup you should not pay to design for scale when creating a minimal viable product (MVP), the least portion of your service or product necessary to test its success before investing further time or money, but you should have a plan in place for scaling when it is needed as your company grows.

Partner Evaluation

Before incorporating a business together, thoroughly test your potential partners. Decide upon a collaborative project to further your business idea, assign tasks according to your individual skill sets, and agree upon a deadline. For example, you could choose to explore the product-market fit for your idea or product. One of you can identify the market, create a test pitch, and cold call several potential customers to gather initial reactions. The more technically skilled potential partner can build a wire frame of how the product will work. How seriously a person takes the assignment and if they deliver it on time will give insight into how they will act as a business partner. Failure to complete the assignment, or excuses as to why it was late, will also enlighten you.

If the collaborative project has a positive outcome it is a good indication of how you will work together as a team. Test yourselves further. Sign up for a hackathon competition if you're techies. If you're not, sign up for a group project that has a factor of intense stress and a deadline such as a pitch contest, business plan competition, or LeanStartupMachine event. See how you react under pressure together. Do you work well together, or does one of you complain while the other works?

Further assessing your potential partner allows you to verify if they're willing to take on the intense workload involved with launching a startup. Ask your potential partner to make 10 customer development cold calls, while you do the same separately. It sounds simple, but the calls are surprisingly difficult and awkward. This makes them an excellent test for dedication to your idea and overall grit. Follow up your calls with a weekend or non-work hour meeting to discuss your findings.

Failure to complete the 10 cold calls and/or being "too busy" for a review meeting are indicators that your potential partner isn't fully committed to the project and will never have the time to do hard projects that are essential to launching a company. A person who completes the calls and comes to a weekend work retreat, however, with detailed notes and the energy to talk about them for hours, shows the drive necessary to be an ideal business partner.

I jumped into a business partnership outside MissNowMrs where I had casually known my partner for a long period of time. While she was an expert in her area of practice, we were not ideal business partners. The stress of a mismatched partnership, and the misunderstanding of the importance of our differing roles, took its toll. The situation, best described as "personally crippling," led me to the difficult decision to leave. I was not always the perfect partner, and I learned that it is important to know when your values and priorities are too dissimilar to have a healthy working relationship. I left a thriving business that I had bootstrapped and built because it was not worth the negativity it was adding to my life.

Learn from my mistake, and thoroughly vet your potential partner(s). A great way to avoid misunderstandings of business responsibilities is to document each team member's responsibilities before entering into a partnership. You can create an organizational chart detailing all of the roles the company will require to run smoothly. Then write the name of the team member or partner responsible for each role on the chart. This clearly defines "who does what." If there are roles left open, you either need to hire a person to fill the open roles or one of your team members or partners must step up to fill the role.

You will never regret the time you spend finding the best cofounder(s) for you and your idea. Syncing with your ideal partner will motivate you in all the right ways. You will be challenged daily to be a better business-person. Equal accountability will motivate you through company failures, tough economic times, and threats from competitors. Having a good part-ner also means that you will be supported during personal struggles and any other negatives that life throws your way.

Are you concerned that a potential cofounder will steal your idea? Since ideas are useless until they are executed, you can protect most potential intellectual property (IP) by primarily discussing the problem your busi-ness will solve. If you do have a "special sauce" that is your key to solving the problem better and faster than anyone else, you can have a potential partner sign a non-disclosure agreement. This agreement allows you to both share your ideas, with the understanding that they will not be shared outside of your potential partnership.

Key Team Members

Recruiting people for a company without an existing product is a challenge. You have to be passionate about solving a problem or challenge that people can understand and own. You have to believe in your idea and be able to rally people around it. Venture capitalist and serial entrepreneur Jonathon Perrelli advises that "creating a cohesive team where everyone shares the vision and has the same values is incredibly important with early hires. These are the people who will help to create your company culture. Joining your company has to be win/win for the founder/team member."

How do you know when to hire a new employee? The timing is right when you have identified a need within your company and you have come across the right person to meet that need. If the need is there and the right person is there, you need to take the risk and hire them. Consider how quickly a new hire will pay for themselves on a 6-month timeline. That person may not be able to cover their salary costs the first month, but if they will make it up in the long run it is time to bring them on board!

When you're not the right person to do a particular task or hold a certain role within your company, have an inner circle of people who will tell you. This allows you to allocate the project or job to someone else. Perrelli believes, "Winning is all that matters and you're not winning if you're in the wrong role even if you think you are supposed to own that specific task."

Who To Hire

A key member to add at your company's inception is a designer. A designer is the team member with the artistic ability to make your product, pitch deck, website, and marketing materials look professional and appealing. Look for a designer who has stellar communication skills along with a portfolio of projects that fit your company's desired style. Recent college graduates or individuals new to the design community are looking to build their portfolios. This makes them eager to join a new company offering multi-tiered design projects, even if you have a limited budget.

Hiring an individual to handle accounting/finance is another must for new businesses. You will need someone strong in projections, numbers, and analyzing markets. They will prove their worth by creating metrics to gauge growth and other company goals. What doesn't get measured and tracked within a company doesn't get done.

Unless you or your cofounder are gifted in the area of communication, consider hiring an individual to handle social media messaging and company content generation. This team member will need to write engaging material for your website, blog, Facebook page, Twitter, SnapChat, and Instagram accounts, as well as come up with concepts for promotional videos.

How To Source Employees

How do you find highly skilled individuals to build your early team? Volunteer at a startup to gain exposure to startup circles. Network at meetups, troll LinkedIn for candidates, and ask experts in the field who they would recommend for your team. Sources for technical team members include Upwork (formerly oDesk and Elance), and Craigslist. The bigger the pool of talent you have to draw from, the better hires you can make. Reviewing resumes and interviewing potential employees, however, can be very time-consuming and exhausting.

Another way to build a productive early team is to hire people that you have successfully worked with already, or hire teams that have worked together on past projects. Having a large startup budget makes it much easier to hire the very best talent for your project. If you are bootstrapping, you will need to get creative on how you compensate your early team members for their time and talents.

Think about what you can offer your early team members. Can employees learn particular skills working for you? Are they able to work remotely and/or with flexible hours? Do you have industry or social connections that could benefit them in a future career step?

If you can find people who share your vision, passion, mission, or cause, they may be willing to work for lower rates to help develop the early phases of your business. Another option is to offer company stock options to offset low salaries for amazing team members.

Is your company making a difference in the world? If so, individuals who cannot quit their day job may volunteer their talents to help you. Volunteers' personal commitment to your mission make them exceptionally well-suited for sales and fundraising positions. The pool of people looking to "do a good deed" is enormous, so advertise opportunities for volunteers to help build your business.

Interns are a fantastic resource for filling skill gaps in your team. Identify areas where you need help, such as design, social media content, sales, or customer support. Then find interns with an interest or background in those areas. Today's college students are aware of the value of startup internship, and will usually work for $10-$20 per hour to secure hands-on experience and build their resume. The true win-win situation is when you hire an intern full-time after they graduate.

Not all positions within your company require full-time employees. There are companies to tap into which offer services like accounting, social media, web development, or product development on demand. You can elect to use one of these companies or subcontract the work to individual freelancers until your business's needs dictate creating a full-time position.

Chapter 4 Takeaways

- Take your time finding your cofounder and make sure that you align on work ethic, goals, and personality.
- Look outside your normal circles for a business partner that has the skills you lack.
- Give your potential partner(s) projects to test their work ethic and ability to hit a deadline.
- Your first few team members are critical to your business's success and culture so choose wisely.

How It Feels

It is incredibly lonely and scary to be a solo founder. It can be done, but it usually feels overwhelming to be responsible for every aspect of your business. The constant pressure of solo entrepreneurship can deplete your creativity and leave you burned out.

Finding your best possible cofounder is magical. You have connected with someone you can trust to handle their part of the business. Someone who sees the vision and will help you make your dream into a reality. It feels like a 500 pound weight has been lifted off your shoulders when you are not responsible for every single thing necessary to survive and thrive as a startup. Someone has your back so you can focus on what you do well, while they focus on what they do well for the betterment of your company.

Further Reading

The Partnership Charter by David Gage

DO THINGS OUT OF LOVE

AND PASSION RATHER

THAN OBLIGATION.

~ IVANKA TRUMP ~

*Elegant*ENTREPRENEUR

OPERATING AGREEMENT ADVICE

Regardless of what planning model you choose for your business, it is highly advisable to create an operating agreement with a designated company attorney. At its most basic level, an operating agreement outlines each partner's responsibilities for running the company, as well as who owns what percentage of the business. It is important to be brutally honest in respect to your abilities and the time you can contribute to the business, as well as your expectations of your partner's contributions. It's easy to say "you do this and I'll do that, and we'll figure out the rest as we go." That laissez-faire attitude has been the downfall of many a partnership, and destroyed amazing ideas before they had a chance to blossom and become successful businesses.

Look at the scope of the project, of building your idea into a business. What needs to be done to get you from A to Z? What timeline are you working on until launch? Do you and your partner(s) have all of the skills necessary to get your idea to launch? Detail exactly who is going to do what, and consider adding a section regarding what happens if a partner fails to perform their duties. It is an awkward conversation that can save you millions in buyout dollars, legal fees, and a lifetime of heartache.

Asking the Hard Questions

Decide how your partnership is going to be divided. Are you equal partners? Are your responsibilities and workloads divided based on equity?

Are capital contributions weighed the same as sweat equity? If you can't agree on how to answer these questions before money and stress is introduced, you should not be partners. Have the awareness and strength to walk away from a partner who may sound ideal on paper, but is not the best match with your vision or personality.

Many entrepreneurs get hung up on the concept that they must enter into a 50/50 split with their cofounder. In actuality, that is rarely a good idea. It is statistically improbable for two people to be bringing exactly half of the cash, skills, connections and/or commitment that a company needs past, present, and future. It is okay for a cofounder to have 20% or less of the business. Work out who is contributing what in terms of intellectual capital, financial capital, business relationships, and ongoing time commitment. Weigh who has what and divide equity accordingly.

You and your partner(s) need to be willing to ask each other difficult questions. For guidance, the 15-question quiz at foundrs.com is incredibly helpful. While the algorithm of the quiz for calculating equity is very accurate, the dialogue is more important. Questions include: "Who had the original idea and told the others?"; "Which founders are working part-time and will join full-time once you get funding?"; "If this founder left, would it severely impact your chances of raising funding?"; etc. Add these questions to your conversation, and come up with your own list. Then, read each question with your cofounders, and discuss your answers.

Voting Rights

Next up, decide upon the voting rights of each partner. Determining who has what amount of say in any decision is essential for the health of your business. Business decisions—both easy and difficult—need to be made expeditiously to ensure that the company doesn't suffer.

Finally, map out the buyout and sellout rules for all partners. This exercise functions to protect the company, the remaining partners, and the partner or partners exiting for whatever reason. No one can predict life circumstances that could cause an unexpected exit. You will be glad to have governing rules should that moment arise within your startup. The undesirable alternative is to create some sort of sellout or buyout agreement with an emotionally charged partner or their family. While potentially uncomfortable, ironing out an operating agreement ahead of time is a key step in business success.

A scenario to consider is what happens if a cofounder has to leave the company after 6 months. A vesting schedule, an agreement that allocates permanent company stock over a specific period of time, will ensure that the company and cofounders are protected if someone cannot continue to contribute as originally agreed upon.

Once your operating agreement is drafted and signed, place it in a safe or safety deposit box and forget about it. It isn't a document meant to be pulled out daily, but to function as a safety net if things go wrong. Use your energy to build your relationships within your partnership and business!

Elegant Insight 4 Takeaways

- Map out all expectations and requirements in your operating agreement.

- If you and your partner or partners cannot agree on duties in an operating agreement, you may need to find new partners to found your company.

- Once your operating agreement is signed, put it away and focus on building your relationships and business.

How It Feels

Writing an operating agreement feels much like writing a prenuptial agreement. Honestly, they both serve the same purpose: ironing out expectations and financials before anything messy or unforeseen happens. Expectations and emotions can make creating this document incredibly challenging. You will feel angry, surprised, hurt, and stressed during the process. Do your best to be honest and level-headed, and ask that your partners do the same.

Consider scheduling several meetings to discuss and agree upon the components of an operating agreement. This is preferable to having one marathon session, and allows everyone time to weigh their options and manage their emotions in a professional way. In the end, you all want to build an amazing company together. This paperwork is a small stop along the way, so persevere through the big messy emotions.

DON'T WAIT FOR THE
PERFECT MOMENT,
TAKE THE MOMENT AND
MAKE IT PERFECT.

*Elegant*ENTREPRENEUR

~ Chapter 5 ~

TIMING YOUR LEAP

You had your ah-ha moment, did your market research and found your cofounder or cofounders that complement your skill set and agree that your idea is revolutionary. You completed your business planning by outlining steps to make your idea a successful reality in the market. You now have the blueprint. It is tempting, in the excitement of early entrepreneurship, to immediately quit your day job and dedicate yourself to making your dreams a reality. Don't do it!

A reality check is very important when timing your leap into the startup world. It is crucial to assess your current situation and take an honest look at yourself and your circumstances. How much money do you have in the bank? How much is your current lease or mortgage? Are you in the midst of a marriage, divorce, or beginning a family? Are you locked into an employment agreement? While conditions will never be "perfect" for your startup, all of these factors should be weighed in the timing of your launch.

Harris, Founder of 1776, advises: "Your timing will be based on some environmental factors, but mainly on your opportunity. If the opportunity for your idea is exploding, you need to jump into the launch of your company to be fast enough to scale before the opportunity is taken by someone else. If your opportunity stems from a personal passion or a gap in the market, it will be easier to dual track (make a living while building your product) and make a go/no go decision based on product readiness." Harris cautions, "It may feel like your idea is tied to an exploding opportunity, but separate yourself and how you feel about your idea.

Sometimes you are not in control of when you take a leap. You might be planning to head in one direction when life throws you a curveball. For example, when I failed to be accepted into medical school after college, life gave me a "shove" into the working world. Leaping (to avoid falling) led to a job selling Canon copiers, which built my foundation of tenacity. Twelve months later, with some experience under my belt, I made a calculated leap. I leveraged my sales knowledge and bachelor's degree in Biology to land a career in medical sales. Once I had a sense of timing on my side, I was better able to examine the various environmental factors for my next move. When you have control of your circumstances you can be more strategic, not only in your timing, but in your career trajectory.

Harris prompts entrepreneurs to ask themselves "What do I need to do this well, not perfectly?" She shares, "In some cases, launching your company is how you test your market. In other cases, you can be more stealthy. Incubators and accelerators can be helpful places to ask for advice. You can ask their third party experts if your market is time-sensitive or if it is okay to take longer to develop your product." Harris adds, "Our job (as an incubator) is to tell you if there is spinach in your teeth."

Some leaps are opportunity and life-stage driven. When I left my role as the number one sales representative for a large medical company to launch MissNowMrs, most people thought I was crazy. What they failed to consider was the opportunity I encountered when my name-change struggles led to the idea of an online name-change service. Research showed that 2.3 million U.S. women marry annually, and 88.6% of them elect to change their names. They also failed to consider the facts that I had sufficient savings to bankroll my idea without jeopardizing my lifestyle, and I was beginning to realize that I could not maintain my current job driving 1,300 miles a week and be the future mother I wanted to be.

Maria Izurieta, a growth-oriented executive who brings strategic leadership to emerging and publicly traded technology companies, is currently the CFO of 3Pillar Global, Inc. 3Pillar Global focuses on helping hundreds of clients build their revenue-generating software products. Izurieta shares her advice for timing a leap into a full-time position at your startup: "Quit your day job when your business can support you in the lifestyle you are comfortable in, and support its own growth." She encourages founders to look at the needs of their company before their own needs. For example, does your company need more engineers before it needs you as a full-time CEO?

From the personal perspective, if you are in a relationship, you need your partner's full support. Entrepreneurship has many perks, but the majority (such as flexible work hours) usually happen later in the growth of your company. It is important to be with someone who has complete faith in you and your idea. This will be the person who will support you in times of struggle, as well as the good times. When you question yourself, your partner should be the one pushing you to make it work.

If your significant other scoffs at your idea or simply cannot provide the support needed to propel you forward, it is time to decide which is more important to you—your relationship or your business. While some partners may "come around" and support you and your idea as it begins to take hold and become successful, many will not. Startups are incredibly hard on relationships: romantic, platonic, and familial. Be aware of the potential sacrifice in relationships you will need to make before you decide to focus and "start up."

Startups & Relationships

Lisa Morales-Hellebo, Executive Director and Cofounder of the New York Fashion Tech Lab, shares her relationship insights from her first startup, Shopsy. *Going through TechStars (a 13-week startup accelerator) as a married woman, I had numerous people asking me how my marriage was doing. I thought this was odd. But then I realized that I was gifted with the exception—not the rule, when it came to husbands. I found out that it is unspoken knowledge that founders end up divorced more often than not. When I thought about why I realized the importance of not only who you choose to marry, but how you both communicate.*

Before founding Shopsy, I was the primary breadwinner in my household so I knew that my husband and I had to discuss the implications of what it actually would mean to go all-in on being the CEO and founder of a tech startup. The conversation went something like this: Are you okay with me going from being the primary breadwinner to likely making zero dollars for an indefinite period of time? My husband unequivocally said that I should go for it and that he had my back. Of course, I was anxious about our finances, but we both figured out a revised budget and committed to making it work, which was amplified in stress by the fact that we owned a home and were parents to our 2- and 5-year-old boys. If I didn't have such a supportive and understanding husband and kids, I never would have been able to take on entrepreneurship, or I would have likely been another divorced founder.

Professional timing is also a key factor in deciding when to launch. You need to be extremely confident in your ability to generate revenue before quitting your day job. If you have a full-time career, there is a need to be very careful with transparency regarding your employer and coworkers. You should not jeopardize your main source of income as you begin the exploration process of an idea. Ideas and entrepreneurs need money as they grow toward a profitable business.

Take some time to understand the moonlighting or outside activity policies of the company with which you are employed. If you signed an initial employment contract, now is the time to carefully review it. Typically, you will be barred from creating a business or service that competes with your current employer for a number of years after you leave the company. The agreement may also state that your employer has rights to any innovation or invention you create while under their employ. Do not risk the nightmare of losing your job and being sued as you launch your business.

From the beginning, be certain to work on your startup during non-work hours. Work on your business during evenings, weekends, and holidays. Never ever send an email using your work account, even to yourself, regarding an idea for your side venture. Consider working part time at your job before you completely transition to running your company full time. Focus on saving money, and try to rein in your lifestyle in preparation for your leap. You do not need to buy new Jimmy Choos when you are contemplating a startup. The savvy entrepreneur prioritizes spending on the items that will make the biggest impact for her company, and wears the heels she already has.

The state of your target market and the economy also play into your timing for launch. Becoming an expert in your market will help you determine the best possible time to launch your company. A good economy means your potential customers have money to spend and a generally positive outlook on spending. Conversely, a recession or depression is not the best time to roll out a new product or service, unless it helps people save money or better their circumstances.

Watching key competitors and their progress in the market can also help you appropriately time your launch. If there is a media whirlwind around the problem your startup solves, or your competitor is failing to satisfy the need for the solution, this is the time to launch regardless of whether it is ahead of schedule.

Understanding any potential purchase seasonality of your target market is another key factor. For example, if you are about to unveil a new tax innovation, timing your release to coincide with tax season is the smartest way to introduce your potential customers to your new solution at the exact moment they need it. Strategic timing is essential to a successful startup launch and early sales.

Knowing the ideal personal, professional, and market scenarios before you make your launch decision will help you make the best possible choice for yourself and your company's future. Be brutally honest and evaluate what you want, what you need to successfully launch, and how you feel about both the upsides and downsides of your startup. When you launch, you need to be completely dedicated to your vision and goals. Zero waffling allowed.

Chapter 5 Takeaways

- Do not quit your day job right away; ideas and entrepreneurs need money to grow.
- Explore the ramifications a startup may have on your relationships.
- Research moonlighting or outside activity policies of the company you work for.
- Understand your market and time your launch to coincide favorably with its demand.

How It Feels

Making the decision to go all in and launch your business is much like the decision to jump out of a plane. There are two likely scenarios:

Scenario 1:

If you have done your research, educated yourself on your market, explored your emotions and commitments, and decide to take the leap you are going to feel like a first-time skydiver. You have most people in your inner circle's support and know that "you can do this." You will feel excited beyond all measure and a little nervous.

Scenario 2:

If you are hasty and just take the leap, you will more likely than not feel like someone jumping out of plane without a parachute. Your parents and friends will tell you not to jump and question your sanity (okay . . . that sometimes happens in Scenario 1). You will feel an insane spike of adrenaline followed by sheer panic and the dread of what will happen next.

Further Reading

The Dip: A Little Book That Teaches You When to Quit (and When to Stick) by Seth Godin

The 7 Day Startup: You Don't Learn Until You Launch by Dan Norris

I FIGURE IF A GIRL
WANTS TO BE A LEGEND,
SHE SHOULD GO AHEAD
AND BE ONE.

~ CALAMITY JANE ~

*Elegant*ENTREPRENEUR

OWN YOUR "ENTREPRENEUR STATUS"

Are you turning an idea or dream into a business and kissing Corporate America or the concept of a 9-5 goodbye? Guess what? You are becoming an entrepreneur. You are joining the ranks of men and women who are shaping our world and changing it for the better, one idea at a time. Oprah Winfrey, Steve Jobs, and Arianna Huffington are just a few of the moguls who share the same title as you.

It is easy to downplay your new entrepreneurial status and say that you are a small business owner or "have a website," but you are doing yourself and your startup a disservice. Those descriptions allow you to stay out of the spotlight and shirk the responsibility of powering or helping power an entire business. The sooner you recognize yourself as an entrepreneur, the sooner you will begin to fulfill the role necessary to build your dream into a flourishing company.

One successful dream builder is Payal Kadakia, Cofounder of ClassPass. Kadakia's company offers fitness fans flat-rate monthly subscription service to participating boutique fitness classes in over 30 U.S. cities, as well as in Toronto, Vancouver, and London. The company was recently valued at over $200 million in a *Wall Street Journal* report, making her a shining star in the world of women entrepreneurs. Kadakia shared her advice for aspiring female founders: "Be true to yourself and surround yourself with positive, supportive people. When I first started out, there were times I would dress or act in a certain way because I thought it was expected of me or that people would take me more seriously. But once I started leading in a way that was authentically me, I really started to see success."

You will need to be smart, driven, creative, and fearless to make your mark and taste success as an entrepreneur. Take ownership of those traits and foster them. Wake up each morning and visualize your goal. Fill your head with motivational quotes and images. Fuel yourself with the stories of other successful entrepreneurs. Learn their success tactics and apply them to your own idea and life.

Immerse yourself in the entrepreneurial culture. Attend networking events and meetups for entrepreneurs in your area, and go with the goal of making friends as well as contacts. Sign up for podcasts interviewing famous entrepreneurs, or subscribe to mixergy.com, which is a site with over 1000 established entrepreneur interviews and 175 courses on learning from entrepreneurs. Also, attend any startup seminars or lectures that pique your interest. The more you learn about entrepreneurship and the more visible you are within the community, the more comfortable you will be with the title and the more support you will receive on your journey to success.

When a stranger asks what you do, tell them you are an entrepreneur. Do not be surprised if your posture and self-assurance improves upon uttering those words. Take notice of a change in that person's demeanor, because you are labeling yourself as a person out of the ordinary, as someone who is capable of the extraordinary. Only 13.8% of the United States population are early-stage entrepreneurs according to the Global Entrepreneurship Monitor.

Introducing yourself as an entrepreneur is also a perfect segue into what your idea or startup is. Be confident. In the startup world, you are your business. If you are not confident in your success, no one else will be. This is not permission to be arrogant, but permission to be honest about your assets and ambition. Tell everyone who will listen about how amazing your idea is and why your company is going to succeed. You need to be drinking your own Kool-Aid before you pass it out to the business world.

As the walking billboard for your startup, it is important to represent it in the best possible light. If you have a meeting, dress well. There may be a whole "jeans and t-shirt entrepreneur" faction out there, but as a new startup founder you need to look smart and on target. A classic business dress will help you look and feel polished, while signaling to whomever you are meeting with that you are someone to be taken seriously. Save the company logo t-shirts for when you are in your office, basement, or gym, not when you are pitching your company to investors or attending a conference.

Own your status as a female entrepreneur. It can feel daunting to be the only person in heels at a networking event or pitch contest, but women-owned businesses are on the rise. The 2012 U.S. Census Bureau's Survey of Small Business Owners for Women[8] was full of fantastic news for aspiring female founders. The survey showed that there are more women-owned businesses than ever before, 9.9 million women-owned businesses, to be exact. That is a 28% increase from the 2007 census. Women-owned businesses employed 8.9 million people, a rise of 1.5 million jobs from 2007. Women-owned businesses also increased their number of employees 20% while men-owned businesses increased their number of employees by only 12%. Use these facts to bolster your confidence as you create your company and own your voice as a female founder.

Katie Orenstein is Founder and CEO of the OpEd Foundation, which is a social venture founded to increase the range of voices and quality of ideas we hear in the world. The foundation's starting goal is to increase the number of women thought leaders contributing to key commentary forums—which feed all other media and drive thought leadership across all industries—to a tipping point. They envision a world in which the best ideas, regardless of where or whom they come from, will have a chance to be heard and shape society and the world.

As a woman dedicated to helping all under-represented people claim their voices, Orenstein weighs in on why it is important for women to own their role as entrepreneurs: "It is important that our voices are heard on all kinds of things. We are all on this globe, what are we going to do with our one wild precious life? Absence of our voices suggests that women aren't entrepreneurs. The kinds of businesses we might start, and how we start them may be different. If we want our interests to be represented and met, we had better be part of the apparatus of entrepreneurship. We need to shape and create businesses and products that meet a need we have or one that we see."

An example of a woman seeing a need and choosing to build a business to make a difference is Elizabeth Scharpf, Founder and CEO of Sustainable Health Enterprises (SHE). While working at the World Bank in Rwanda, Scharpf learned that female employees were missing work regularly and 50% of girls were missing school because of menstruation. The reason: sanitary pads cost more than a day's wages. Sharpf was outraged at the injustice, and felt compelled to do something about the issue. She founded SHE to help women jumpstart socially conscious businesses to manufacture and distribute affordable menstrual pads. Through Scharpf's social entrepreneurship efforts and health education and advocacy, girls and women in Rwanda will lead even more productive lives than before.

Elizabeth Scharpf's 5 Steps to Grow Your Social Enterprise:

1. **Do Your Homework**—Get all of the facts around the problem and the population it affects.
2. **Become Legitimate**—Create partnerships with large universities and companies.
3. **Rally a Great Team**—Add members with valuable skills to make measurable results.
4. **Get Wins, Re-Up**—Create a long-term plan with short-term goals along the way. It shows progress to investors and brings internal team morale up.
5. **Get the Big Tuna**—Take your social success and replicate it around the world.

Enhanced by your own unique perspective of the world market, do not be afraid to interject thoughts from your female perspective. Emphasize that being a woman equips and qualifies you to be an expert in your niche or startup field. It is the variety of our thoughts and skill that birth new ideas and products to make the world a better place.

Another key to owning your entrepreneurship role is to position yourself as an expert in your industry or business niche. Why should the public listen to you? The simple answer is because you know more about the problem your service or product solves and the customers that use it than anyone else.

No one is born an expert. It takes personal experience, research and massive amounts of customer interaction and feedback to become an expert. For example, when I founded MissNowMrs I did not have a book resource titled "How to Disrupt the Renaming of Yourself After Marriage." Instead, I studied journal articles on name-change sociology, combed census reports for name change statistics, called every DMV in the United States to learn their name-change procedures, and interacted with early MissNowMrs customers to understand their state and county-level name change laws and loopholes to slowly become an expert and began positioning myself as such.

The results of positioning myself as an expert were immediately beneficial to MissNowMrs. National and local television appearances to discuss married name change, writing articles for *Huffington Post Weddings*, and offering quotes included in countless media articles built credibility and brand recognition for my company, which resulted in increased sales. Consumers assume that anything in the media is legitimate and that credibility sells products. I also benefited from positioning myself as an expert. The more I was contacted by the media to provide name-change insights, the more confident I felt as an expert and young female founder.

[8.] 2012 U.S. Census Bureau's Survey of Small Business Owners for Women: http://nwbc.gov/facts/new-fact-sheet-women-owned-businesses

Elegant Insight 5 Takeaways

- Embrace your new identity as an entrepreneur and immerse yourself in the culture.
- Power dressing: make your message a professional one.
- Your unique viewpoint allows you to make a difference in the world.
- It is okay to emphasize that being a female entrepreneur benefits your business.
- Become an expert in your industry or business niche.

How It Feels

Joining any new group can make you feel nervous. It is especially difficult to compare yourself to the famous faces you associate with the title of entrepreneur and then identify yourself as one of them. You may feel downright fraudulent for a few weeks, but the more time you spend working on your idea and the more entrepreneurial events you participate in, the more you will feel like you can wear the title.

Owning your entrepreneur status is incredibly empowering. It validates you and your efforts to create something new. You should be very proud of yourself and the personal growth you have achieved so far in your journey to becoming an entrepreneur. You should also feel excited for all of the adventures and experiences left to come!

NEVER STAND BEGGING

FOR THAT WHICH YOU

HAVE THE POWER TO EARN.

~ MIGUEL DE CERVANTES ~

*Elegant*ENTREPRENEUR

~ Chapter 6 ~

FUNDING

Do you want to build the next Google, Facebook, or Tesla? Is your passion to be a billionaire on paper with a 1% chance of getting there? Or do you want to create cash flow, lifestyle flexibility, and be your own boss? How much money do you have and how long will it take your business to start generating positive cash flow? Your answers to these questions will help you determine the best way to fund your startup.

According to Amy Millman, founder and president of Springboard Enterprises, "Entrepreneurs need to know their control profile." How much you want to control your business dictates where you should source your funding. Millman continues, "Know yourself; if you want to do it all don't take outside investments." Any wisdom Millman shares should be trusted: 590 female-led companies have participated in Springboard's accelerator programs, raising $6.7 billion in funding, creating tens of thousands of new jobs, and generating billions of dollars in annual revenue since 2000.

Starting a company requires cash. If at all possible, opt for the internal/founder funded route, where you (and any other founders) provide all of the funding for your business. It may be painful and leave you eating ramen noodles for months, but you will remain in control of your vision and all the decisions concerning how you grow and where you go. A survey showed control of their company is important to female founders. Ninety percent of the founders of the 50 Fastest Woman-Owned/Led Companies[9] funded their businesses through family, friends, and personal fortune. These women did not want to lose control to venture capitalist investors, so they did not solicit venture capital firms for funding to grow their companies.

Bootstrapping

Bootstrapping your business will also keep you hyper-motivated to succeed in order to feed yourself and pay your rent or mortgage. Your objective should be to grow your company until it is "customer funded" through sales revenue. This may sound obvious, but it is a concept that is often ignored or overlooked in the startup world these days.

Do you use your savings, drain your IRA, personally borrow money on credit cards, take a second mortgage on your home, ask for money from your parents, or take out personal loans? These are tough questions about money that need to be answered before you can fund your business. Banks are unlikely to offer you a loan to launch a startup, so you must determine the best source or sources of cash to get your idea off the ground.

Be creative about your beginnings. You do not necessarily need office space or a fancy desk. Think about where Mattel, Apple, and HP began . . . all in a garage. The important thing is to identify the steps necessary to go from idea to income, and then take those steps methodically. As an entrepreneur, don't be afraid to trade or barter for the things you need to succeed. Swap marketing advice for coding or a vacation home stay for graphic design work. You have to be scrappy and humble to self-fund a venture (unless you have a trust fund).

There are alternatives to funding your business, but each comes with a price.

Family and Friends

The first step of outside investor funding is soliciting your family, friends, and closest contacts. Do not be afraid to ask the people who love and believe in you and who have the chance to benefit from your success for capital to fund your dream. Create a legal contract for the family funding you receive. It will prevent bad blood over unrecorded, but "remembered" details. The contract will also serve as a reminder to family members that they have invested in you and your passion. This is the point when people "invest in your company" not just loan you money. Still feeling shy about asking for money? Consider the point that your family and friends may be upset if you do not give them the opportunity to help you by investing in your company.

Outside Funding

The next step outside family/inner circle investor funding begins with working the circuit and being on the startup scene. Make sure that your business plan is polished, your logo and business cards look professional, you own your web address (domain), use the associated email address, and have an elevator pitch you could chant in your sleep. Then start signing up for business plan competitions, pitch contests, accelerators, grants, prizes, incubators, Lean Startup Machine workshops, and Startup Weekends.

Exposure at these events is key to getting a proper seed round, or initial outside investment, for your business. Prove your team FIRST . . . with a pitch contest win or hackathon win or similar social proof points. Team is what matters even more than your good idea. Virtually no venture capitalist backs a solo entrepreneur. Do not jump into a seed round if you do not have a killer team . . . period.

Meredith Fineman, Founder and CEO of FinePoint, works with women to teach them how to brag, redefine self-promotion, and create a vocabulary to speak positively about their professional achievements. As an expert in the field of self-promotion, Fineman has advice for female founders in pitch contests and investor meetings: "It is essential to pitch yourself along with your product. Be positive about your accomplishments. It is not bragging if it is something you have done—it is a fact. The most outgoing CEO always wins."

Investor Requirements

Most outside investors require four basic components for a business to be deemed worth investing in. The components are: team, market, product, and traction. If your company lacks any one of those four components, the opportunity to invest in you will not be as attractive to investors.

Entrepreneurial winners grasp both the best timing, as well as the best funding options. If your business needs to scale quickly, funding is a factor that directly and positively affects growth. Alicia Robb, the Senior Fellow at the Kauffman Foundation, shares that "women use less financing and less outside financing than men. If we can get them over the funding hurdle we will have a lot more high growth businesses with female founders." The startup ecosystem is exploding with more female focused funding options than ever. Below are a few of my current favorite female founder funding options.

Accelerators:
MergeLane
NYFT Lab
Springboard
The Vinetta Project

Online Platforms:
EBW2020
Moola Hoop
PlumValley
Portfolia

Angels:
Astia Angels
Broadway Angels
Golden Seeds
Next Wave Ventures
Pipeline Angels
37 Angels

Venture Capitalists:
Merian Venture
Rivet Ventures

Grants:
Huggies Brand: Mom Inspired Grants
InnovateHER: Innovating for Women Business Challenge
The Eileen Fisher Women-Owned Business Grant Program
Wal-Mart Women's Economic Empowerment Initiative

Seed Funding

Seed funding rounds are all about building relationships with accelerators or Angels and Angel networks. Springboard Enterprises, AngelList.com, and OneVest are examples of networks that could provide your company with its first professional round of outside funding. Most seed rounds involve convertible notes from investors.

A convertible note is a loan that can be converted into stock at the time a company can be professionally valued in the market. Typically, early investors or Angels will lend your company money before either of you know how fast or far your business will scale. For example, if an angel loans you $100,000 and your company is later valued at $1,000,000; the Angel can convert their loan into 10% of your company's stock.

Words of wisdom from Millman for women pitching for a seed round: "Value your time and value you when asked how much you have invested in your company. So many women say they have not invested anything when asked, discounting hundreds of hours of research and work. This immediately lowers the valuation of their company." This harkens back to owning your role as an entrepreneur. Pitching is not the time to be humble about your company, contributions, or ambitions. It is the time to own it and sell it.

Timing, when you seek funding, is also very important. Janet Van Pelt has held chief executive roles for the past 20 years at both public and private technology companies. As the founder and CEO of CourseMaven, a suite of software as a service solutions enabling access and completion for post-secondary learning, Van Pelt , believes that too many companies rush to secure funding before they are fully prepared. She shares, "You can only walk down the stairs to the prom once, so don't waste that opportunity. Your company only gets to be new once in the world of investors." Van Pelt also cautions founders about funding. "The concept of seed capital is smoke and mirrors. You need to have a business plan, revenue model, customers and a plan to scale. You're raising money to implement your plan, not explore your idea. When you raise money, you put yourself on a clock.

You need to have a good path to a potential exit for your business to keep your investors happy."

Lettered Funding Rounds

A Series A investment is the first significant round of capital financing from venture capital firms. This round is usually in the form of preferred stock, which is stock that includes an option for the holder to convert the preferred shares into a fixed number of common shares, typically any time after a predetermined date. Series B rounds, and further lettered rounds are the consecutive rounds of capital solicited to finance your company's growth via investments from venture capitalists or private equity firms.

Morales-Hellebo, of the New York Fashion Tech Lab, shares her funding advice stemming from her experience as the founder of Shopsy. Launching a contextual search fashion platform, she faced an extra set of barriers as a female founder, minority, and solo entrepreneur, making her insights particularly important. According to Morales-Hellebo, "The popular concept of building something awesome, get paying customers, talking to inventors, and millions will come to you isn't true. Focus on building a solid business. If you are looking for funding, don't fish in the ocean, fish in a barrel. Look for investors who have invested in female-founded businesses and your industry. Don't be delusional, be purposeful."

Morales-Hellebo learned from her hard knocks from Shopsy "dying on the vine" due to a lack of funding and lack of investor understanding of contextual search, and turned that failure into the vision that created the NYFT Lab. The Lab's mission is to connect key level fashion executives with startups that are developing technologies that are valuable to them. They collaborate on a three month partnership to get a pilot of the technology up and running (a scenario that would have allowed Shopsy to flourish). Nineteenth Amendment, a fashion startup in the inaugural class of NYFT Lab, made retail history when they inked a partnership with Macy's less than a year after they launched. This partnership illustrates the value of Morales-Hellebo's vision to give fledgling fashion tech companies the support necessary to succeed.

Grants

Business grants are an alternative source for funding. As a female founder, you have an edge in the entrepreneurial world. There are grants created specifically to help women-owned businesses. The beauty of grants is that you are not required to pay the money back. The downside is you have to research which grants you qualify for, apply for the grants, win against competition, and report back on the way you used the grant. The process may sound daunting . . . but we are talking about free money to grow your business! As you begin to look for female founder grants, it is advisable to start searching at the state level. This is as simple as typing your state + female business grant into a search engine. Another excellent resource for grants is the United States Department of Commerce Minority Business Development Agency, or mbda.gov. Use their website to search for grants for women in business.

Crowdfunding

Crowdfunding is another outside funding option that has expanded into two basic categories: traditional and true equity. One of these sources may be right for you and your business.

Traditional crowdfunding such as the sourcing done through Kick-Starter and Indiegogo initially started as a way to pre-fund a project, but now serves as a litmus test for product/market validation. Even if you do not need the money, you can find out if the market exists for your idea and receive customer validation before you make the leap into entrepreneurship. Using one of these platforms as a test is a great way to know and show you can make it as well as to amass facts to use during pitches and presentations.

True equity crowdfunding, another alternative, is just becoming legal through Title 4 of the Jobs Act. This is where platforms, like OneVest, can help founders solicit for investment dollars in exchange for equity in your company. Their purpose is to help you find people who will invest in your company, immediately.

Tanya Prive, cofounder and CEO of OneVest, shares her thoughts on how crowdfunding is changing the landscape of funding. "Crowdfunding is democratizing access to capital. You no longer have to go to Harvard or Ivy League schools to have the connections and network to get funding. Funding is moving from a boys' club network to a merit-based selection process."

When asked how OneVest specifically benefits female founders, Prive explains: "Offline, women don't have as much funding reach as men; online there is more opportunity for them. OneVest supports women from a growth point and investment perspective. Women reach more potential investors with less effort using an online platform like ours." OneVest participants also benefit from the company's "hands-on" approach. Founders are given access to literature, training programs, and events to polish their pitches before they are positioned in front of investors."

A word to the wise: new legislature and technology are combining to lower the barriers to entry for creating and funding a business. These changes blur the lines between traditional funding rounds. The legal costs, mechanisms, and availability to reach investors have changed with technology and so the startup world is again changing. What remains constant is that you can seek funding when your company needs it, but only when it is needed based on your company's current market value.

Chapter 6 Takeaways

- Know your entrepreneurial dream before you consider soliciting investment money.
- Money is never free, and outside investments are the most expensive money you will ever borrow.
- If you want to impress potential investors, place emphasis on your team and their skills.

How It Feels

Elise Whang, Cofounder and CEO of SnobSwap, just wrapped up a million dollar plus investor seed round. She was kind enough to share her candid thoughts and emotions about the funding process. Whang says, "Having to ask or pitch for funding is one of the hardest things to do; I felt like I was holding my hand out for money. It is important to remember that you are not just asking for money - you are offering an opportunity to have an impact on your business and receive financial gain."

When you take on investors, it is really exhilarating. You have people who believe in you, your team, your business and your vision. On the other hand, there is the fear of disappointment in not meeting their expectations. Whang believes that, "Fear can be repackaged into a motivator." Fear helps her work incredibly hard with her team to meet her goals and move the needle. Fear feeds the thought that there is no room for failure and fuels the mission to succeed.

Prior to her fundraising journey, Whang was afraid she would give up too much of her business to gain capital. But, as she wisely surmised, "One hundred percent of nothing is nothing." Whang challenges entrepreneurs to think about it this way: is it more important to own 100% of the business or to grow the business? That contemplation will make the decision easier.

Investors do not have to solely have the role of financial beneficiaries. Whang's thoughts are, "If you have investors that are advisors or strategic partners, it's like winning the lottery! Not only do they have skin in the game, they sincerely want to help you succeed and have the ability to do so. If you're successful, then they're successful. Your interests are totally aligned."

Further Reading:

A Rising Tide by Susan Coleman and Alicia Robb

[9.] 50 Fastest Woman-Owned/Led Companies of 2015 list: https://www.womenpresidentsorg.com/news-events/50-fastest-growing-women-owned-led-companies

CONTINUOUS IMPROVEMENT

IS BETTER THAN

DELAYED PERFECTION.

~ MARK TWAIN ~

*Elegant*ENTREPRENEUR

~ Elegant Insight 6 ~

CUSTOMER FUND BEFORE YOU'RE DONE: PEOPLE WILL BUY IMPERFECT THINGS

Most non-entrepreneurs believe that a product or service must be perfect and completely functional before it is brought to market. As women, many of us feel that we were trained to be perfect from birth and the thought of not putting our very best foot forward is shocking. Guess what, in business, and in life, you need to get over the concept of perfection, and work toward embracing what you have. Then, strive to constantly improve upon that.

Customer-funding your startup as soon as possible is paramount to building a successful business. It supplies capital for the continuation of growth for your business. Also, obtaining customer funding will be tangible proof and confidence that consumers will purchase your product or service. Satisfaction and pride comes when your company begins turning a profit and is funding its own growth. It is one of the best moments in entrepreneurship.

Izurieta, CFO of 3Pillar Global, Inc., encourages entrepreneurs to approach their customer base with the most rudimentary version of their product. She advises, "Get valuable customer feedback before pouring money into fully building your product. If you fully build a product and go to market, you will most likely have a miss. Your miss alerts competitors to the need in the market and allows them to build a competitive product while you are fixing yours." Izurieta observed, "Building in stages allows you to stealthily be first to market with your idea successfully."

When I launched MissNowMrs.com, it did not match my end vision for the product. Our service only auto-completed the four federal name-change forms and the state driver's license form. Frankly, I was scared to serve up my idea and company before it was fully built with all state-level forms and notification letters for creditors. Would customers feel ripped off and dislike the service? Would we get bad press before we even got the full product off the ground? But, realistically, I needed to prove to myself and my partners that customers would buy an online name-change service before we put any more time, money, or research into the company.

Within 30 minutes of turning on Google ads, my first customer, Wendy (I will never forget her name!) purchased my name-change service. It was incredibly validating to have someone see the value in the service I created enough to purchase it. With the site launched and advertised, I performed test marketing. This determined exactly what our customers wanted and what they would pay for my service. We started with the service priced at $39.95, but soon discovered that when we dropped the price to $29.95, it became an impulse purchase and sales skyrocketed.

With money coming in from customers, I was able to fund research for additional product expansion and hire someone to handle customer support. Then I could focus on company growth. Brainstorming to boost sales, I came up with several variations of the service to offer clients. One variation offered a basic name-change account that only included government forms for $19.95. Another variation—a complete package that had all forms and notification letters for $29.95—was offered with the thought that our customers would appreciate a choice. They did not. The basic-package customers did not think they received enough for their money and the complete package customers did not think the notification letters were worth the extra $10.00 when they compared the pricing. Offering only the complete service for $29.95 turned out to be the money maker and the sales platform MissNowMrs used for the next seven years. Analyzing MissNowMrs customer purchase behavior allowed me to hone the exact product-to-price value proposition the market responded most favorably to, which set the pricing model for the burgeoning online name change industry.

Customer-funding your startup creates a customer base actively using your product or service. It is a great perk! These customers are invaluable to you and your company because they can, and will, find bugs in your system before you do. They will also ask for innovations you would not have thought about. Or their requests will confirm that your next product improvement is right on target. Customers will also use your product outside the scope that you envisioned and help you broaden your market. Best of all, some customers will become brand advocates for you.

Note that with the early releases of not-quite-perfect products and services, there will be complaints. How you handle customer complaints and feedback will determine the success of your company. You can be indignant and sweep negative reviews under the rug, or you can actively survey your customers and request feedback. Everyone wants their voice to be heard, so reward suggestions on product issues from your clientele. Most likely, they want to help you and your fledgling company instead of flaming you on a review site. You will also be able to nip small issues in the bud before they become media or industry headaches.

While handling customer feedback, remember that there is always a "percent dissatisfied." No matter how many improvements you make or how hard you try to make every single client happy, there will always be a small group of people who remain unhappy. This is true in all industries and in all societies. Understanding that this group exists can help ease the anxiety of negative comments and allow you to prioritize which customer feedback to give your attention.

Refunding the "percent dissatisfied" is the easiest way to placate them, and avoid further negativity. MissNowMrs has taken the Nordstrom approach to refunds, in that we want all of our customers to be happy and if they are not, they receive a full refund. Several irate customer complaint calls have been defused with a refund. And, surprisingly, many refunded customers appreciate our customer service to the point where they tell us they will recommend MissNowMrs to friends that could use it.

If you are selling a tangible product, it may be too costly to give refunds to all customers who complain. You should create and publish a refund policy that is fair and will keep your company in the black. If you treat your customers with respect and listen to their needs, they will remember the great customer service more than what they disliked about your product. Bottom line: customer goodwill is essential in today's connected world of reviews and recommendations.

Tracking your refund rate month over month and recording the reasons for refunds is a great (and free) way to keep your fingers on the pulse of your customers' needs and pinpoint when and where you need to improve your product or service. When you see a spike in refunds, it is time to devote attention and company resources to repairing the issue in question.

Elegant Insight 6 Takeaways

- Customer funding is the ultimate funding available to startups.
- Customer feedback is gold and should be viewed as opportunities to improve your product.
- The "percent dissatisfied" exists; refund them and move on.

How It Feels

Much like a performance review that comes with some constructive criticism, hearing anything negative about an idea you have built from the ground up will naturally make you feel defensive. If you can remove yourself and your emotions from the critique, you will be able to look at complaints and suggestions as opportunities to learn about your customers' needs. View the feedback as opportunities to improve your product or business. It may still sting to read a bad review, but if you can learn from it, it is well worth the emotional turmoil.

I AM SEEKING. I AM STRIVING.

I AM IN IT WITH ALL MY HEART.

~ VINCENT VAN GOGH ~

*Elegant*ENTREPRENEUR

~ Chapter 7 ~

BUILDING YOUR PRODUCT

Building your idea into a minimal viable product can be fraught with challenges. Whether you are creating a tangible product, an online service, or an app, one of the biggest challenges entrepreneurs face is how to communicate their ideas in a relatable and concise manner to the outside world.

Many entrepreneurs struggle with getting their idea out of their brain and onto paper, into a physical prototype, or expressed via web code. But you must create something tangible to communicate your idea with others. If it is a product idea, start with drawings. Move to CAD/CAM 3D designs and send your design to a 3D print shop for prototype creation. If it is a web or service-based idea, build a basic website with SquareSpace, Wix, or Shopify. Once you have a prototype of your idea, collaborators have something to relate to, expand upon, or improve. Prove you are committed to making your idea a reality; most people simply wish their idea would work without applying effort.

An early example of achieving success by creating a prototype from a product idea, is the story of the PDA (Personal Digital Assistant). Jeff Hawkins was one of the creators of the Palm Pilot in the late 1990s. He was faced with the daunting task of creating a handheld electronic device that synced with a computer and helped users access their calendars and personal contacts. With no technology for the project available, Hawkins whittled a prototype PDA out of wood and walked around with it in his shirt pocket. Having a tangible object to represent his idea allowed him to interact with his "PDA." It eventually helped him narrow the options of what size batteries and screens could be used in the creation of the electronic version of the PDA. These decisions propelled his idea forward to the working electronic PDA, which created a billion dollar industry.

When asked what the most challenging obstacle she faced while building her business, Payal, the founder of ClassPass, says one of her most challenging obstacles she faced while building a business was grappling with how to invest her time and resources. "When I first started Classtivity [the initial company that became ClassPass], I was really concerned with how our site looked. It ultimately had to be completely redone and that set us back in many ways. In thinking back, I've realized the most important thing is just to get your product out there into the market to see what people's responses are. I've been working on this company for almost 5 years, and we have had to pivot a handful of times before we got it right. But for me, I was always determined to succeed. I think as an entrepreneur you have to think that way—you can't be scared of failure. I'd rather run straight into my fear to figure out what's next versus not acting at all."

This book is an example of how putting an intangible idea on paper helped transform it into a reality. For over a year, the concept for a female founders guide to startups was in the back of my mind. Finally, I created a Google document and began writing down my ideas for insights and chapters. When the document grew from 2,000 words to 20,000 words, I felt confident enough to write a book pitch and ask my graphic designer to create a sample book cover. Suddenly the idea was tangible! At that point, armed with a digital summary complete with professionally designed cover, I was able to approach and solicit interviews from prominent entrepreneurs to add their wisdom to this guide.

Physical Product

Creating a prototype of a physical product may seem impossible, especially if you do not have a background or skill set in product design or manufacturing. Fortunately, there are many resources available to walk you through this process.

Step one is to create product sketches and a list of functionalities. Next, find an industrial designer to listen to your product description and functionality needs. Together you can work to design drawings or a 3D rendering around a product that meets manufacturing standards, just be sure to create a written agreement giving you full ownership of product rights before you get started. Where do you find an industrial designer? The Core77 Design Firm Directory allows you to search by the type of professional needed, their location, and even the size of your design budget. You can also search through the listing of the Industrial Designers Society of America to find industrial designers in your state.

Once you have a professional design, you'll need to find a company to manufacture a 3D printed model or a functional prototype. Thomasnet.com is a resource for entrepreneurs looking to fashion a prototype. Use them to select what service you need, such as plastic fabrication. Submit your request for quotation (RFQ) and you will be matched with up to five shops that can quote a price for building your product. Industrynet.com is another resource available to search for prototype manufacturers.

If you are creating a prototype of apparel accessories, furniture or home decor, MakersRow.com is a website that allows you to search for American factories within your industry. Makers Row was cofounded with the goal of empowering those with "just an idea" to begin creating their own products. So it is an ideal starting point in your search. Askwear.com is another resource for entrepreneurs in fashion. They will assist with everything from pattern design to manufacturing 50-piece prototype orders of a specific garment.

Service-Based Product

Service-based products have the allure of being relatively easy to create and take to market. Typically founders are familiar with the service they have or want to offer, so it seems reasonable to build a business around their knowledge or skills. When you are creating a service-based product, you must build a model and processes to ensure that your customers receive the same stellar experience through your service each time they use it. Your business is the process; it needs to be extraordinary!

It is important to realize that your business is not you and what you are personally able to do to satisfy your customers. Your vision and personal energy propel your company's growth and innovation, but you should not be the sole source of power or fuel. Instead, your business is creating a documented step-by-step process that ensures your company provides your customers with a valuable service that is consistently excellent. You will need to establish each aspect of your business then you will need to think several steps ahead and create detailed operating manuals for employees. The reason these manuals are done in the early stages of product development is because training and understanding of these manuals, and the processes involved, will not only position your employees to succeed, but it will allow you to fine-tune your product and see how it will work from start to finish. Your goal is to create a business that runs like a machine, without your constant assistance. This frees your focus for high-level goals and prevents burnout.

There may be technology efficiencies in your service business which can only be achieved by building your own software. Work out the manual processes first, then fine tune them before implementing the ideas for a software product, as outlined below.

Be aware of the trap of underpricing your service product. On the surface you may be able to offer a service for much less than the current market rate. However, keep in mind that you need to allow enough margin to run all aspects of the business. For example, you may work for an accounting firm and realize that you can process an individual's taxes for half of what your employer charges. If you created a competitive company charging half the standard rate for tax preparations, you would certainly have an influx of customers. But if the customers are paying exactly what it costs for you to process their taxes, there won't be any profit left to pay for office space or the Internet bill, or someone to answer the phone.

As a founder, your role and focus should be directed at improving your process and increasing sales. The service needs to be priced in such a way that the company generates enough cash flow to pay employees to do the work, while you focus on improving your process and increasing sales. Because customer satisfaction depends on the quality of service they receive, invest time in educating and training your employees.

Software Product

A huge challenge faced by entrepreneurs with a software idea but little technical experience is garnering knowledge from their sketches, wire frames, and functional requirements to know what coding platforms are best suited for building their product. The best way to figure out what you need is to request quotes to build your idea from several local and offshore development firms. As you review the quotes, ask what platform technology each bidder would use for the project and why. There may be a 10x difference in quotes, but that doesn't matter. You are compiling ideas and platforms to build your product. The technology most mentioned is typically the platform you should go with. That being said, deduce the reasoning behind the different platform recommendations to make an educated decision on what technology you will use. Often the less expensive solutions can get you to market, while a more expensive platform might help with more advanced services or scaling your company later. Understanding the tradeoffs and costs associated with building your initial product, versus building for future goals, is essential as you make your platform selection.

According to Mike Bradicich, Vice President of Day1 Solutions, "Knowing the code platform you need will help you select the right developer for your project. It's like knowing if your construction materials are wood or steel so you know which to hire: a carpenter or a welder." Now that you know the coding platform that is perfect for developing your product, it is time to find a developer with skills in that platform. Ways to source developers include attending meetups for that platform, using CoFoundersLab, MyStaffNow, TopTal.com placing a Craigslist ad, or searching Upwork (formerly Elance and oDesk).

How do you know if you have selected a good developer? Test them. Give your new developer a small piece of the project, including not just design work but also business logic, and give them a deadline to complete the project. If the developer dodges communications, delivers late or doesn't deliver the project, look for a new developer. If they are responsive to emails and deliver the project on time, take their work to a trusted Chief Technical Officer (CTO) for a review before hiring them for the full project. Where do you find a CTO? Look through your LinkedIn contacts and ask your friends. You can offer to pay the CTO you find for a two-hour to half-day review of the completed development project. CTO hourly rates can range from $75 per hour to $250 per hour, but it is well worth your investment to know whether you have found a great developer and can trust them to complete your project in a professional way or if you are being scammed.

Security features are something to consider as you design and build your product. Have a CTO advise you on security measures for now, and later, or at a minimum, run a McAfee vulnerability scan of your product to have any issues pointed out.

Creating a software product is a multistep process. First, brainstorm a list of all of the features you want your product to have and prioritize one or two features to construct your minimal viable product. Next, use a wireframe tool like Balsamiq to map out how the software features will work. Make sure that the final wireframe covers all of phase one. Now is the time to loop in a graphic designer to make your product engaging and user friendly.

Decide which platform your software is intended for (i.e., where does it work?). Options include box software (CDs or downloads you purchase for your computer), web software, and phone software.

Now that you have a minimal viable product wireframed, a design of what the finished product should look like, and know your programming technologies, it is time to develop the product. If you have a technical cofounder with strong management skills, you can consider hiring in-house developers, subcontractors, or look into offshore options. If you do not have a technical cofounder, go with a design/build shop to have your idea developed. You will have the advantage of working with people who are designing something that they can build within your budget, instead of designing something gorgeous that is impossible to code.

Phone App Product

The more integrated smartphones become in our day-to-day lives the more opportunities arise for creating apps to solve problems. As of June 2015 there were 1.5 million apps available through the Apple Store and 1.6 million apps available through the Google Play Store; competition is fierce. Your app will need to be spectacular to succeed in such a marketplace. If you are ready to turn your idea into a spectacular app, there are a few different ways to go about creating a minimal viable product.

The least expensive way to tackle creating an app is to build a website that renders on smartphones. If you want to go a step up from that, you can build an app that renders your website. It will look better than just a website and you can market it through the Apple Store. The third choice for creating an app minimal viable product (MVP) is to code for cellular devices using a single set of code. The last option for creating an app is to do platform specific coding. You should select one phone platform for the app to work on (iPhone vs. Android vs. Microsoft) and then use that MVP to determine if you want to code for the other platforms.

Phonegap is a form of code which allows you to develop an app that runs on all three mobile platforms: iPhone, Android and Microsoft. There are limitations to the features, design, and performance functions you can use the code for, but it is a fantastic way to build a minimal viable app for all three platforms.

Logo and Website Design

Now that there is a prototype of your idea it will be easier to create a brand around it. The hallmark of your brand is your logo. It will be on your website, marketing materials, and any product packaging. Unsure of exactly what you want your logo to look like? 99designs.com is a service that asks you a few questions about your idea/business and your preferred style.

They then send your logo request out to their network of professional designers. You will receive dozens of logo designs and have seven days to ask for changes and tweaks. At the end of the week you select the logo you love and pay $299 for it.

Once you have a logo you can use the colors and style of it to inspire a coordinating website and blog for your product. Do not make the mistake of thinking that consumers will infer the value of your service or product. Spell it out plainly on your home page. As you design your website, remember that a picture is worth a thousand words. Consumers do not take the time to read . . . they barely skim before deciding to buy or not. Find a way to present your product or service and the problem it solves graphically. You can use those graphics not just on your site, but on social media and in advertisements.

Key components of an effective website typically include a clear call to action, testimonials, video(s) and a simple design. A call to action is telling consumers what you want them to do. If you want them to sign up or purchase, make that option available on your home page as text or a large button. Testimonials from your current customers immediately build trust with consumers. It is important to showcase testimonials that spell out why your service or product is amazing as well as any that overcome buying objections a new customer might have. For example, if you are concerned about the price of your product use a testimonial similar to this: "This service saved me so much time I would have happily paid double for it!" Short videos can be used to augment testimonials and to demonstrate how your product or service works. As you build your website, resist the urge to over-design it. Simple websites are appealing to consumers and do not dilute your messaging.

It is critical to have a website that scales to size correctly for viewing on computers and mobile devices. If you do not have a mobile-friendly site, you are missing out on 40-50% of the market searching the Internet. Millennials use their phones for everything, especially shopping. Do not miss out on sales because your website is clunky, be sure to select or ask for a responsive website design.

Curious if your website is communicating the message you want it to? UserTesting is a company that has real people use your website and records their real-time reactions on video. It is amazing what you can learn from a few individuals' initial and unbiased thoughts as they encounter your product or idea for the first time. Use their feedback to fine-tune your site before your product launch.

Protect Your Product

As you build your product, a small amount of preventative effort can save your company from theft of your intellectual property (IP) and the creation of copycat businesses. Identify what is unique to your product or service and collaborate with your business lawyer on the best ways to safeguard it. Legally protecting your idea and your investment after countless hours of research, validation, and creation of your product or service is imperative as you go to market.

Adding terms of use to your website is an inexpensive way to safeguard your product and any intellectual property you have created from copycats. Intellectual property includes any unique creations, such as code, a particular process or mechanism, or artwork you have created, which has commercial value. Require users to check a "terms and conditions" box before they purchase or use your product. They must agree to the terms you have created with your attorney that verify users will not steal your intellectual property and use it to create a competing company or they cannot access your product. Professionally constructed terms and conditions hold up in court making them well worth the monetary investment. Looking for inexpensive legal advice? Many universities with law programs offer free legal consultations, so look for one near you.

Purchasing domain names surrounding your website name is another efficient way to protect your company. The small expense of purchasing the .net, .org, .co domain suffixes of your business's URL is worth making it more difficult for competitors to use your name to steal your customers and web traffic. It is also wise to purchase a few domains that include the best key words for your product to further protect your product's Internet presence. For example, as the founder of MissNowMrs.com I own every website URL with name change and married name change that I could purchase to hinder new name-change services attempting to find a website name in my niche.

Copyrighting your written work is another way to protect your intellectual property. Technically, you can claim copyright to your unregistered work as soon as you create it and post it as copyright protected. However, having a registered copyright with the United States Patent and Trademark Office provides established financial recourse in case of infringement. You can file copyright registration yourself, but the process is complicated. It is usually easier to have an attorney file on your behalf.

A patent establishes intellectual ownership of an invention. You cannot patent an idea. Patents cover inventions or processes, not the ideas that inspired them. To successfully apply for a patent, you will need to illustrate exactly how your invention works and explain how it is different from previous, existing inventions. Working with a patent attorney is the fastest way to begin the patenting process. But be forewarned, it typically takes 32 months for a patent to be approved by the United States Patent and Trademark Office.

An understanding of your company's strong and weak legal defense points can help you develop security systems that safeguard your IP, and/or create future products that are more legally defensible. For example, my knowledge of MissNowMrs's vulnerable internal account data resulted in the creation of a security mechanism that locks users' accounts after more than 3 state forms are viewed. This mechanism prevents extensive theft of our form data and alerts our team that someone may be trying to mine our IP. It is imperative that you keep a close eye on vulnerable areas within your product or service.

Chapter 7 Takeaways

- Building a prototype is the best way to communicate your idea and polish your product.
- There are resources available to create any kind of prototype.
- Legally protect your product to prevent IP theft and copycat companies.

How It Feels

The feeling tied to the experience of taking an idea and turning it into something tangible is joy. You have created! Now you have a new way to communicate your product to others so that they can understand it and your vision for it. Being understood is incredibly affirming, especially if you spent an extended period of time creating your prototype.

The process of investigating legal options available to safeguard your product can be tedious, but the security it produces is well worth the effort. The knowledge that you have done your best to protect your product or service will provide a satisfying level of peace and comfort in the emotional whirlwind of building a company.

Further Reading

Hooked: How to Build Habit-Forming Products by Nir Eyal

The Lean Startup by Eric Ries

SMALL DAILY
IMPROVEMENTS ARE
THE KEY TO STAGGERING
LONG-TERM RESULTS.

*Elegant*ENTREPRENEUR

HAVE A GOOD IDEA DAILY

The "big idea" that launched your journey into entrepreneurship is paramount, and it should be one of your main areas of focus. But companies and entrepreneurs that kick back after the "big idea" get left in the dust of innovation and competition. To make your business successful you have to nurture it with a minimum of one good idea per day.

In the early phases of forming your startup generating daily ideas will be very easy, since you are building something new and constantly reconfiguring your idea as you map out how to make it work. As you continue to build your company it can become more challenging to come up with ideas. If you are searching for inspiration, it is helpful to think about each aspect of your startup individually and in minute detail. Think of your company in separate segments so you can concentrate on forming ideas around each segment. The usual company segments are: your product or service, how your product or service is used, communicating with customers and advertising, website, and potential partners. Every startup is different, so you may need to add more segments to make this list complete for your situation.

Spark Ideas About Your Product/Service:

How could you improve your product dramatically?
How could you improve your product minutely?
Who would benefit from the improvements?

Would the improvement help you target a new audience or market?

Would the improvement be something customers would pay more for?

Would the improvement be something current customers could pay to "add on?"

If you could wave a magic wand, what do you wish your product could do?

What do you wish your product could do better or faster?

How does your product look? Does it need to be updated or could you offer customization?

Would you buy your product immediately or would you have to think about the purchase?

What would incentivize an immediate purchase (scarcity, coupon, flash deal, lower price, testimonial)?

Is your product or service credible?

What makes your product better than any others attempting to solve the same problem?

Is something too slow or confusing about your product?

How can you better explain the confusing part?

Spark Ideas About How Your Product/Service is Used:

How does your product or solution make your customers feel?

What benefits do your customers receive when they use your product (outside the solution to their problem)?

Are your customers using your product or service the way they are "supposed to?"

Is misuse a problem or an opportunity to expand your market?

Do your instructions ensure that your customer will be able to use your product easily the first time?

What do you hate about your product or service?

What does it currently fail to do or deliver?

Is there a way to let your customers try your service or product before they buy it through a sample or use of a small portion of the service?

Spark Ideas About Communication with Customers/Advertising:

What do you think is the best part of your product/service?

Are you effectively communicating the best part(s) to your customers?

Can you explain exactly what your product or service does in a graphic (most customers don't take the time to read)?

Can you summarize the problem your product/solution solves in a meme that has the potential to go viral?

When and where do your customers experience the problem you are solving?

Are you targeting your marketing to that specific time and location (be it a place or situation in life)?

Is there a way to buy a list of customers in the specific time and location you are targeting?

Are there other companies that provide a service at the same time and location for your customers?

What are methods or avenues of advertising they are using?

Is there a way you could work together?

Are you everywhere your customers are looking for a solution?

What annoys your customers?

Who/what do your customers not like or not want to be like?

Is there a way for you to position your product as a way to help customers not be like something they don't like?

Spark Ideas About Your Website:

Does your website clearly define the problem and solution?

It is easy to understand how your product works/solves the problem?

Is the value of your product or service clearly explained to the end user?

Is it easy to purchase on every page?

Is there a call to action on every page?

What are the top three reasons someone wouldn't purchase your product or service?

Can you address those three reasons to overcome them?

Is something on your website hard to read or difficult to understand?

What pages are your customers on when they abandon your website?

Is your website mobile traffic friendly (i.e., what does it look like on your phone)?

Potential Partners, Affiliates, or Acquisitions

Ideas about potential partners, affiliates and acquisitions can be elicited by thinking about which companies advertise to the same customer base or are in the same industry or niche as you. You may be afraid to think of large companies as partners for your startup in fear that they will steal or copy your idea/solution. In most cases, large companies are not nimble enough to copy or steal an idea. In fact, they are usually open to partnering to use your idea or product to benefit themselves and their customers. So put the big names down on paper along with medium and small ones; they all count as ideas and you can "work up to them" if you need to build some confidence.

Spark Ideas Specific To Each Potential Partner Or Affiliate:

What makes your service or product a perfect fit for them and/or their customers?

Why would your idea or product be an added value?

Is there a way to bundle your service or product with theirs?

Could they market your service or product as an upsell?

How much of a revenue share are you willing and able to offer?

Is there a way you can send your customers to them?

Do they have a pain that your company can solve?

How can you use your partners' needs to create the perfect pitch?

What do you do with ideas about companies who compete with your startup in some way? Keep those ideas and expand upon them! They can turn into a list of potential companies for you to acquire as you grow (especially if they have or do something you don't). Conversely, the list of competitors can be used as potential purchasers to shop your company to when you are ready to exit (especially if you have or do something they don't).

Major Ideas vs. Minor Ideas

As your company launches and begins to grow, it can be easy to get caught up in brainstorming major ideas that will make a huge impact on your company and revenue. To be honest, major ideas are expensive to execute, take a great deal of time and effort to deploy, and are risky. Do not discard major ideas that pop into your head, but also avoid causing an internal log jam in your brain by focusing solely on generating them.

I adore little ideas and details, and fortunately so do consumers. Minor ideas can end up causing major results and typically do not take the time and cash that major ideas need to be implemented. For example, I had the whim of adding a running bluebird (from our logo) to draw attention to the Get Started button on the MissNowMrs purchase page. Customers were charmed, and our conversion rate increased 2%.

It is important to recognize the need for daily good ideas, major and minor, and foster their creation. Set aside a minimum of 15 minutes each day to clear your head and think about new ideas. This 15 minutes does not have to be while you are sitting at your desk. In fact, I find that my best ideas happen when I am at the gym or in the bath tub. Disconnecting from your office can allow you to shake off startup stressors and let your imagination play.

Encourage your partners, friends, and employees to share their ideas with you. Create a culture where great ideas are expected and celebrated. Consider rewarding any employee's good idea with a coffee or gift card. Solicit customer feedback to generate even more ideas, and reward them with a discount or a simple thank you email from you. The more you foster the generation of ideas, the more ideas you have to work with, which betters your chances for successfully growing your company and achieving your dreams.

Take the time to log the daily good ideas you and your team come up with. This allows you to look back on days that are lacking in inspiration. Ideas that seemed far-fetched a few months ago may be perfect for your business now, or may spark even better ideas that will help you continue to build your business. With the speed at which technology is changing, impossibilities yesterday could be possibilities next week. Remember, a dearth of daily ideas creates stagnation, which can paralyze your business's growth and inhibit its trajectory to success.

Elegant Insight 7 Takeaways

- Constant good ideas are necessary for the health of your business.

- Segment your company into small sections to generate questions that beget good ideas.

- Solicit ideas from everyone in contact with your company.

How Does It Feel

As the source of the "big idea" your business was built around, you will feel responsible for keeping that idea alive. It is stressful to pilot a new company, and stress can kill creativity. It is easy to get discouraged and feel like you are floundering for a growth strategy. You can feel like you are failing to lead in the area of innovative thought.

Allow others to help you generate daily ideas. This solution will decrease the anxiety you feel and has the additional benefit of diverse thinking and problem solving. New ideas, no matter how small, will energize your thought process around company issues and help you come up with new ways to grow and improve. When a small idea turns into a product extension or marketing coup, you will feel elated and more confident in yourself and your company's success.

SHE WHO
DARES WINS.

*Elegant*ENTREPRENEUR

3 . . . 2 . . . 1 . . . LAUNCH

You experienced the problem, developed the idea, worked on the solution, formed a company and built a team. Phase one of your product, which is commonly known as a minimal viable product, is established. This is it! You are ready to orchestrate your launch!

Pre-Launch

Alpha test first. Alpha testing is comparable to the application of rough grain sandpaper to smooth out glaring product defects. Test your product on yourself, any cofounders and team members, and use it as a customer would. Be brutal in your testing notes. When MissNowMrs underwent Alpha testing, a friend uncovered a major flaw. She pointed out that there wasn't a place to enter a previous name if you had been married before or were adopted. The system had been created around my experience as a woman changing her maiden name after marriage, so the questionnaire asked for the user's maiden name and married name only. You may not have the funds to address all of the identified issues all at once, but knowing the issues to change is valuable.

Beta test next. It is smoothing out smaller product defects with fine grain sandpaper. This phase of testing includes offering free downloads and trials of your product to attain real-world exposure and usage. Ask users for honest written feedback and remove yourself during the trial. Unfiltered user experience is vital to your product or service becoming a success. Early users will identify flaws before you introduce your product and begin charging for it.

Using Beta Testing Feedback to Improve a Product Pre-Launch

Andrew Smith is Senior Vice President and Chief Product Officer for Platforms at MicroStrategy, a leading worldwide provider of enterprise software platforms with high profile clients including Facebook and Starbucks. Smith shares his insights on the importance of incorporating feedback from Beta testing into product revisions before they are launched.

Engaging with customers early and frequently is vital when launching any product to market. Whether the engagement takes place through usability-focused Alpha design sessions, Beta testing, limited rollouts to select customers, or other methods, having these interactions will enable your organization to validate the value proposition, firm up the go-to-market strategy, identify and kill critical defects, and make quick tactical changes as necessary before launch.

Not all customer conditions can be created within the technology laboratories and not all possible interactions with the system can be predicted ahead of time. Especially with larger pieces of software, one of the biggest advantages of Beta testing is that you will receive direct feedback from scenarios that are difficult to replicate or from user interactions that the team did not anticipate. For example, perhaps the product team believed that a certain data import functionality would only be used to pull in small spreadsheets for analysis, but discovered through Beta testing that a number of customers actually found this functionality so useful they wanted to import very large spreadsheets containing all transactional records for the company and the system crashed when they tried to do this. Without this feedback early on, the team would have launched, system uptime would have been compromised, and customers would have been less than enthusiastic about the new offering.

Consider the cost of making changes in the software world. The implications of bad design or a bug in the software sneaking in are much greater as the team moves through the development life cycle. Traditional project management teaches that if a change costs one hour to fix in design (modify the wireframe, mockup, workflow on a piece of paper, or storyboard), the same change will cost 10 hours to fix in the testing phase once implemented and can be over 100 hours to fix once generally available on production systems.

Traditional "waterfall" software development tries to attack this problem with a rigorous design and review process up front to detail out every last pixel of the product. This makes the specifications very clear but can be a big investment and the risk is that requirements that were initially perfectly validated by your customers are obsolete by the time the implementation, testing and push to production have been completed. Congratulations, you shipped the right product but you were late and customers have already moved on. It can be hard to catch up again.

Modern software companies use product development techniques such as Agile, focusing on rapid delivery of the highest business value items first. Stakeholders from within and outside the company collaborate to define a set of functionality for a minimum viable product, which is then taken by the development teams and broken up into a series of "iterations" or small chunks that typically last two weeks where the output of the cycle is fully tested and stable. Doing so results in software that can be delivered to customers every two weeks for feedback and validation. At the start of each iteration the priorities are re-evaluated and if new requirements have come in the team has a chance to react to those changing conditions. The team can constantly adjust along the development path, avoid wasted effort, stay closely connected to customers and ultimately ensure their delight at launch.

Pre-build a Community

The next step is to market your company. Start email lists, a Facebook page, and build a social media presence for your company. Begin writing blog posts about your product/service and industry so when the masses begin to search for your product, your articles will appear in search engine results. Join LinkedIn groups and professional groups to establish credibility and contacts within your industry. Develop your customer base so when the launch begins you are positioned for rapid growth. Use contacts from your KickStarter or Indiegogo campaigns to build your community. Procure early testimonials to bring affirmation and life to your website and social media (consumers love testimonials).

Remember, if you have to delay your launch to alter a few user interface issues, it is worth the credibility you save. The goal is success. The courageous entrepreneur will solicit, synthesize, and absorb the necessary feedback for continual product improvement.

Launch

How do you alert all of your potential customers about your amazing product or service debut so they can purchase it? The answer is marketing. Marketing will become your main focus as you launch.

Marketing is every effort you make to promote your company and sell your product. Jerome McCarthy came up with the Four P's of marketing in the 1960s that are still used today. The Four P's are: product, price, place, and promotion.

Product

A product is the item that satisfies the needs or demands of your customers. It can be a physical product or a service. Each product has a life cycle: introduction, growth, maturity, and eventual decline. Considering the length of your product's life cycle will help you anticipate and problem solve for each period. For example, if you are building an iPhone app consider the window of time you have to build it and how long it will be relevant to consumers before it is replaced by new innovative solutions.

Price

Price is the dollar amount a customer pays for a product. The price you set for your product determines the amount of profit you can make on each sale. There are several factors that affect the price that you select. The most important factor is that your customer deems your product's value exceeds its price. Once you know what your customer will pay to solve their problem or need, you must decide if you are going to match your competition's price, undercut their price, or price your product higher to highlight its superiority for your customer.

Place

Place is where you sell your product to customers. Convenience is key. The more convenient the place for your customers, the more likely they are to buy. For example, think about the candy placement in the grocery checkout lane. Determine if you should sell your product online, through wholesalers, in a catalog, in stores, through partners, or a combination of these options.

Promotion

Promotion is all the methods you use to communicate to customers and partners the value of your product. This is by far the largest and most important P of the Four P's of marketing. I have broken it into several segments.

Traditional Promotion

Traditional advertising methods include print ads in magazines, newspapers, billboards, etc. The tricky part of traditional advertising is that it is an expensive method with a limited scope of readers, and it can be very difficult to track the results. If you pay $2,000 to run a magazine ad, how do you prove that the ad drove enough sales of your product to cover its cost and turn a profit? New media or electronic media, such as Internet banner ads, paid search, and sponsored blog posts have infinite reader reach and are easier to analyze. You can use tracking links and promotional codes to mark which customers came through the specific ad or posts.

Promotional collateral is your printed material, which includes the design and printing of business cards, flyers, postcards, stickers, t-shirts, banners, pens, and any other items emblazoned with your logo. These items are a direct reflection of your company, so they need to be well-designed and of high quality. It is important to find a professional designer with whom you work well and can afford. A great production source for quality printed items is GotPrint.com. Their prices, low minimum print quantities, quick turn-around time, and customer service are all stellar. When you are considering the design of your print items, remember that they are created to sell your product. This sounds simplistic, but if your website, phone number, and email aren't on the item with your logo, how will potential customers find you?

Direct mailing postcards is a great way to promote your product, especially if you are a local company or brick and mortar business. The U.S. Postal Service has a program, Every Door Direct Mail, which enables entrepreneurs to send mailings by postal routes. This program, for approximately half the cost of regular postage, utilizes targeted zip codes to reach potential customers with your marketing materials. Please note that there are specific postcard size and print requirements to be met when you use Every Door Direct, so reference their website before you print your postcards.

The direct mail alternative to Every Door Direct Mail is mailing postcards to specific individuals. This method involves building, purchasing, or leasing a list from a list broker. The postcards are addressed and labeled by you, or by a printing service, before they are mailed.

Postcards are a great way to advertise because a customer has eye contact with them while sorting the mail. Postcards have a 100% open rate, yielding an opportunity to capture consumer interest with an engaging image or logo. Tracking the effectiveness of direct mailing campaigns is difficult unless you offer a coupon code or personalized URLs (PURL). The code identifies which customers purchased your product as a result of receiving a postcard. However, you run the risk of having the coupon code posted on the Internet for everyone to use.

Online Promotion

The Internet has revolutionized the way entrepreneurs reach their customers. As consumers use search engines, they see ads and suggested websites relevant to their search keywords. Keywords are exactly what a person types in when looking for a product or information. Example: The keywords "100% organic pet food" will source a list of websites and companies that offer organic pet food.

Your company has the opportunity to promote its product to consumers through paid ads with Google and Bing/Yahoo. Use their ad creation tools to craft your marketing message. Then, decide which search words are most effective to display your ad. The payment platform allows you to bid on any keywords you want for ad promotion. Multiple companies bidding on the same keywords drive the bid price up for your ad to appear when those specific words are searched. You only pay when someone clicks on your ad, and you only pay just higher than the next highest bidder (not your maximum bid). You will need to determine what pay-per-click price is profitable for your company on each set of keywords you choose to bid on.

Internet search results can also promote your website free of charge. Search engines want to deliver exactly what their searchers are looking for, so they constantly monitor websites for keywords and links from other websites. Simply put, the more times keywords appear on your website, the higher the search engine will place you in its organic search lists. Inbound links are links from other websites. Search engines consider links from reputable sites as votes for your content. The more prestigious and relevant the site linking to your site, the more valuable the link is in raising your search engine results. Websites at the top of organic search term lists receive massive amounts of free traffic from search engines.

Search Engine Optimization (SEO) is the strategic use of keywords to bump up the ranking list of organic sites associated with a set of keywords. Make a list of the keywords and phrases your customers would type into a search engine and use them often on your website and blog. Be cautious not to dilute your marketing message by overusing keywords. Another way to engage SEO is during the process of titling and writing blog posts for your company blog. Search engines consider each blog post a new page on your website. The more pages your site has with keywords, the higher it will be ranked by search engines. So regardless of whether it's 10 or 10,000 people reading your blog, it is an essential online marketing tool for your company.

Social Media Promotion

Social media marketing is the hot new way to reach potential customers. Creating and engaging through company Facebook, Twitter, Pinterest, Snapchat, and Instagram accounts should be a priority. These accounts allow you to promote your business and personally interact with your potential customers. Instead of a single piece of printed collateral, you have endless comments, posts and pictures to create a personality for your company and attract a following of people who want to interact with you and your brand.

Elizabeth Shea is Founder and CEO of Speakerbox Communications, a public relations firm that helps its clients achieve their business goals through creative strategies in messaging, media and analyst relations, thought leadership campaigns, content marketing, digital marketing strategies and more. With over 18 years of PR experience, Shea shares her thoughts on the importance of professional, smart social media when women are representing their business, "There are blurred lines between personal and professional social media. You need to be authentic in all social media channels and get over yourself." She advises women to see and be seen in professional and industry settings. "The more photos you have in professional environments with industry leaders, the more you and your company are recognized as part of that ecosystem." Shea shared this tip for new entrepreneurs, "Attend an event where an industry influencer is speaking and then write about what you learned in a blog post. Email your post to the influencer, and they will typically share it on their social media and boost awareness of you and your company. You can also ask to take a photo with the influencer and tag them in the photo on social media to show your connection to them and again increase your company's connection to the industry."

Avoid being sales aggressive on your social media accounts. Social media posts should be on par with cocktail conversations about your company. While you can and should promote your product and its features, no one wants to be constantly inundated with buy this, buy this now messaging. The more you can engage your followers with your social media accounts, the better. Consider offering a prize for the best photo posted with your product, or the best video testimonial. Consumers enjoy winning prizes and appreciate a variety of content—even content that is not generated directly from your company. Authenticity is always rewarded, so stay true to your company's mission and use social platforms to build communities that support your product.

Social media platforms are ever-evolving ways for businesses to pay for exposure to new customers. These platforms have incredible amounts of information about their users. You can benefit from targeting a very specific age group, in a specific location with interests related to your product. Try to schedule a call with each social media platform's marketing experts (some are easier than others to reach). These experts can co-create a profitable campaign in a brief period of time, and will also reach out to you when new marketing tools become available. Most advertising platforms offer credits such as first $50 free to help you get your campaign off the ground, so you don't waste money as you learn.

Email Promotion

Email marketing is another way to promote your product to the masses. Companies like MailChimp, Vertical Response, and Constant Contact make it simple to create emails to market your product, upload email lists, and manage which emails go to which lists. These companies also have built-in software to track the number of people who open your emails, and any links that they click on, so you can pinpoint what is and is not working.

When crafting an email to potential customers, engaging graphics and brevity are essential. The most successful campaigns have a witty subject line that prompts a consumer to open the email. When opened, a simple yet enticing visual message and a specific call to action, such as a prominent buy now button, appear. Test several subject lines to see which one has the highest open rate. Split your list into segments and send each segment with a different subject line. Do not be afraid to continue experimenting with subject lines as your product and customers change.

Event Promotion

Trade shows, conferences, and industry events present multiple benefits to new companies. First, they offer you the opportunity to be face-to-face with hundreds of potential customers, sell your product, and do product research simultaneously. These events also give instant visibility and credibility in your industry with both customers and other companies in attendance. First impressions are important. It is worth investing in an eye-catching set of banner stands or a pop-up booth display, professional literature, and enough staff to handle questions. Capitalize on the opportunity to form personal relationships.

When MissNowMrs first launched, I invested in a gorgeous tradeshow booth that made the company seem much larger and more established than it was. While exhibiting at a bridal show in my hometown, I connected with a woman who was working in the David's Bridal booth. She mentioned how nice the MissNowMrs booth was, and agreed to pass on my information to the head of corporate partnerships within her company. This brief first impression and interaction resulted in an eventual long-term partnership between MissNowMrs and David's Bridal, the largest bridal-store chain in America.

In the excitement of attracting customers and establishing your company within your industry, do not overlook potential partners also exhibiting at events. Yes, every exhibitor present is a possible partner for your company. Make a point to introduce yourself and exchange business cards with all of the companies at the show. If additional information is requested, be sure to email them within 24 hours of the show's end. Follow your email with phone calls to your best leads.

Marketing is a huge growth and visibility driver for your product, but it is also a large investment of your time and budget. It is important to quickly pinpoint what marketing is working and what isn't so you can allocate funding. Adding a space for customer response as to how they discovered your company on your checkout page or cart is a great way to review which marketing efforts are working, which are not, and which are new avenues to pursue.

Pre-Professional PR

Your company's launch is a great opportunity to generate press before you can afford a professional PR firm. Provide detailed information to local publications and community bloggers about your launch. Most are looking for leads on new businesses, products, services within their customer base or area, and will seize the opportunity to announce a new company in the community. Communicate with any ties to academic or professional publications; this is the time to share your new company and intended launch date. Always include a photo of yourself, your company logo, and a bulleted list of facts about your company. You may not get an interview, but the information may be kept on file for a future article related to your business.

Remember, you can have the most amazing revolutionary product or service, but if people do not know about it they cannot and will not buy it. You are only as good as your marketing plan and execution, so do it right.

Chapter 8 Takeaways

- Use feedback from Alpha and Beta testing to improve your product, even if they slow your launch.
- Pre-build a customer community to maximize your launch success.
- Marketing quality and intensity will directly affect your sales and business growth.

How It Feels

Preparing for the launch of your company is an emotional roller coaster, simultaneously exciting and a little terrifying. Detail upon detail in a time frame called "rush!" There are so many details that you want to make perfect and so much to do to ensure a great launch that you can get caught up in the insanity and miss a major moment in your life, and your company's history. Take time to absorb the enormity of this step and the fact that you have made great progress from your initial idea. Congratulate yourself and your team for their hard work and dedication.

As you officially launch, embrace the adrenaline rush that comes with this achievement. It comes from showing your idea to the whole world and waiting for their reaction. It is completely normal to oscillate between thinking "They love it," "They hate it," "This is the best thing I have ever done!" and "What have I done?" It will take time to analyze the market response to your idea, so instead of obsessing, break out the champagne and celebrate this victory for your idea and team . . . you did it!

Further Reading

Search Engine Optimization All-In-One For Dummies by Bruce Clay

Hack The Bird: Advanced Twitter Playbook by Adam Khan

Guerrilla Marketing For [choose the subject you need]
    by Jay Conrad Levinson

Traction by Gabriel Weinberg and Justin Mares

BE PRETTY IF YOU CAN,
BE WITTY IF YOU MUST,
BUT BE GRACIOUS
IF IT KILLS YOU.

~ ELSE DE WOLF ~

*Elegant*ENTREPRENEUR

SET THE TONE FOR YOUR CORPORATE CULTURE—NEVER LET YOUR MOOD DICTATE YOUR MANNERS

Impeccable manners are the hallmark of class, and allow their owner to navigate difficult situations with grace and tact. Manners are a veritable coat of armor against emotional outbursts that can cost one dearly during pitch contests, staff meetings, and partnership negotiations. Should you be passionate about your startup? Absolutely. Should you let your emotions interfere with your work or cloud your judgement? Absolutely not.

Passion for your startup is incredibly valuable, but must be bridled to be effective as a founder. You can completely disagree with a judge or potential investor's stance on your idea, but blasting them with your gut reaction will immediately alienate them and anyone in their circles of influence. You can always agree to disagree, and then examine the "opposing party's" suggestion. There is value in any opinion, even if it is unfounded, and understanding their viewpoint will make you stronger. You will become better prepared to explain your company and market more eloquently to any like-minded individuals in the future.

My personal observation and belief? You might not be able to control how smart you are or how attractive you are, but you can control how polite you are. Manners open more doors and opportunities than you can imagine; often manners are completely neglected by the majority of people in the business world. You can be hell bent, forceful, or intimidate people in order to grab what you need to be successful, leaving a trail of wreckage behind you. Or, you can be gracious and genuine in your quest for success and be esteemed as an exceptional businesswoman.

This is your project and your company. You make the choices and rules. You set the standard to build the corporate culture that you desire and thrive in. You can choose to show grace to all of your team members and create an open culture of politeness where an idea is heard from start to finish, no matter who is talking. This choice of environment encourages innovation and motivates employees to strive to make a difference in your company. While politeness is essential, do not allow yourself to become a doormat. Strive for the golden mean, the desirable middle between two extremes. Be polite, but also be effective in your authority to run your business.

Leslie Bradshaw, the managing partner of Made By Many and a self-described battle-tested innovator, operator, leader, and growth-driver, shared her thoughts on creating a corporate culture of civility, dignity, and respect. "Employees will work harder and smarter and be loyal to someone who values them. You get the best out of people when you have mutual respect. Execution of an idea comes down to people. If employees are not treated well or heard they are deincentivized, and will take their foot off the gas. You need every person on your team using 100% of their gas to get your idea off paper."

You also have the power to hire qualified women of any age to work for your business. Your college-aged social media maven may help your company go viral, while you help groom her into a future entrepreneur or venture capitalist. Other women who work with you will have a respect for entrepreneurship instilled in them for life. An example of female foundered company prioritizing hiring women as employees is Rent the Runway. The company has 500 employees, 70% of which are female. The "Boys Club" has been around for ages; it is about time we had a "Girls Club" for women at the top to help other women on their climb upward. Strive to build a culture that helps build strong women and inspires them to start their own businesses.

Another key component of a thriving startup culture is diversity. Hiring team members of different ages, cultures, sexes, and work experiences will give your company an edge in selling to the world market. Diverse teams are strong teams. A team that combines a host of varying backgrounds and opinions generates many more possible solutions than a team of the same people sharing the same points of view. From personal experience I can say that when I sit down with my CTO and Vice President of Marketing at MissNowMrs, we come up with solutions that none of us would have arrived at on our own. The company and our customers benefit from our united diversity to solve a problem. Dawson, founder and CEO of The Vinetta Project, believes in the value of diversity in a company's culture. She advises founders, "Be intentional and strategic when creating diversity in your company. Designate money for recruitment and development of your desired culture."

Diverse minds help solve problems, one diva in charge does not! Every entrepreneur wants to have the absolute best team working together to make their dream a reality. A diva attitude virtually guarantees that even if you have a great staff, they will be looking for a new boss as soon as they understand the diva type they are employed under, or when opportunity knocks (whichever comes first).

Do you want to keep your employees and foster a company culture that encourages loyalty and a strong work ethic? Toe the line personally. As a founder and/or CEO, become the best example for those who work with you. Focus on productivity, give 100% of yourself to your work, finish projects ahead of time, ask for feedback and actually act upon it. In other words, model the behavior you wish to see those around you emulating. Everyone is watching you and taking cues, whether you want them to or not. Best business practice is to cue your way to company-wide success and avoid long lunches and shopping trips on the company time or dime.

Setting the tone for dealing with setbacks, both business and personal, as a startup founder is essential to the success of your enterprise. An anti-diva can take a horrible mood or day and use her angst to power through projects instead of venting on innocent coworkers. Do not enable would-be divas with complaints or snide comments. Instead, channel frustrations into the energy that overcomes obstacles and finishes projects. Problems are not an excuse for inactivity, they are a source of innovation and accomplishment.

Elegant Insight 8 Takeaways

- Manners matter . . . period.
- Choose to create a corporate culture that supports and empowers women.
- Diverse teams result in more varied and better solutions to problems.
- Set the tone for your company culture by embodying the person you want all of your partners and employees to be.

How It Feels

Handling a difficult situation with class feels amazing. As you review the incident in your mind, you can take pride in handling yourself with positive eloquence and know that the other individuals in the situation respect you and your company, even if they disagree with your viewpoint.

Manners are the wall between what you rashly think and what comes out of your mouth. Hone them and you are a force to be reckoned with in business, as well as all aspects of your life. Have you ever heard of an entrepreneur who was too polite? Conversely, have you heard of a diva entrepreneur or mouthy mogul? Which do you think is respected and inspires others to emulate?

ASK YOURSELF IF WHAT
YOU'RE DOING TODAY
IS GETTING YOU CLOSER
TO WHERE YOU WANT
TO BE TOMORROW.

GROW...FAST

Your company looks bigger, when it is bigger. Now it is time to focus on growing swiftly but steadily. Consciously take time to brainstorm ways to grow your business. How do you find more customers, partners, and extensions of your brand? What can you do to build your brand's recognition? How can you improve your business 1% today? Finding the answer to these questions will propel you and your company towards growth and success.

Growing a business is all about sales. Do not make the mistake of confusing selling with marketing. Marketing can assist in sales, but they are two entirely different processes. Sales is the action of selling something for money; your company needs money to fuel its growth.

Revenue Generating Strategies

There are three basic strategies for generating revenue: acquire more customers, acquire more money from each customer transaction, or acquire customer loyalty and increased purchase frequency. Each strategy is detailed in this chapter.

Increase Your Number of Customers

The first revenue generating strategy is very simple: an increased number of customers directly increases your number of sales. Purchasing lead lists to actively call and email is a fast way to boost your customer base and profit. You can also provide customers with a discount for referring a friend to exponentially grow your customer base without spending a dime. These efforts in conjunction with your marketing initiatives will help increase your number of customers and thereby increase your company's sales.

Increase Customer Spending

Now that you have invested time and money into increasing your number of customers, it is essential to groom customers to increase their spending when they purchase from you. More customers spending more dollars equals more money for you to use to grow your company through product improvements or hiring more staff.

The easiest way to entice customers to spend more money is to offer them more items or upgrades to purchase. Once they have their wallets open, give them every opportunity and incentive to buy more. If you are selling a product, offer an add-on that improves the product for the customer. If you have several add-ons, consider offering a discounted bundle price (less than purchasing the add-ons separately). Add-ons and bundling also boost sales for online services. Consumers love special offers. Every extra dollar you earn enables your company to fund profitable growth.

Increase Purchase Frequency

The final strategy for making money is getting your customers to return and purchase more frequently. Adding an auto-billing or subscription payment option for your product or service is a guaranteed way to ensure customers purchase from you on a weekly or monthly basis. Reminder emails or thank you calls that detail the benefits of your product or service, as well as any new updates or upgrades, are another great way to keep your customers purchasing regularly.

Companies based on one-time-use services struggle with this component of the strategy, but can usually gain additional sales by offering a gift version of their service. Gifting is a way to approach a one-time use customer for an additional sale, and of course those sales add up to more money for your business.

The Importance of Sales

I cannot overemphasize the importance of sales activity in growing your business. Former president of IBM, Thomas Watson says, "Nothing happens in business until a sale is made." If you think about it, nothing is manufactured, shipped, or used until it is sold. In a bootstrapped startup, no one gets paid until a sale is made. Your company does not need a technical support person or team if nothing has been sold to support. Selling your way to success is your only option besides failure. Internalizing this concept and making certain your team internalizes it will fuel the fire to sell your product or service. After all, we all want jobs and income, right?

Selling involves interacting directly with your customers. Smile and dial (pick up the phone) to convince the person on the other end to buy your product. Afraid they will not want to buy? This is your opportunity to learn and overcome sales objections. Each call you make will become easier and easier as you fine-tune your presentation and product offering. Direct selling allows you to directly impact your company's bottom line.

Consider creating a sales funnel of customers. A sales funnel tracks customer progress from initial contact to purchase, and allows you to visualize where each customer is within the sales process. Customers you know nothing about and have not contacted go into the top of your funnel, or universe. As you qualify customers you place them in the descending 90, 60, and 30 days from purchasing stages of your funnel. You can customize funnel stages to match the timing of your sales cycle (some may be longer and some may be shorter). The value in sales funnels comes from devising ways to move each customer closer to purchasing your product, being able to forecast future sales, and having a consistent visual reminder to backfill your universe with new customers.

SALES FUNNEL

Universe

90 days

60 days

30 days

customers

Commit yourself and your team to selling. It is incredibly easy to hide behind your marketing efforts to avoid the discomfort of direct customer contact. You cannot fall into that trap and grow rapidly in a highly competitive information-fueled market space. When you are tempted to redesign your ads or website to boost sales, stop and think about what action you can take to better sell exactly what you have. Strive to focus on directly persuading your customers to purchase your service, or work with partners to have them sell your product or service.

Strategic Partnerships

Strategic partnerships with established companies that have brand recognition, a built-in customer base, and complementary products or services are another way to grow. Who are the industry leaders in your space? What companies have customers that are your company's ideal customers? Read every industry publication available. Look to source potential partners from the article authors, as well as from the companies paying for print advertisements. You should also attend industry tradeshows, conferences, and events to find potential partners in the exhibitors. The bigger your initial partners, the larger your company looks by association. While size is not everything, it certainly helps to look big and lock up key partnerships before your competitors can.

Once you have identified the companies on your partner wish list, it is time to formulate the ideal mutual value proposition. What would make a large company want to partner with you, or share their customer base with you? Consider what you have to "trade," it is not always solely revenue. For example: Are you an incredibly hip product that would be a perfect add-on for an established, slightly old-fashioned company? They may be trying to update their image, making you a perfect potential partner. Do you interact with your customers right before a potential partner's product is sold to them? If so, your customers may be a perfect customer or sales lead for that partner. There are endless ways to work with other companies. Finding a way to fulfill one or more of their company needs, while they fulfill one or more of yours, is key to a profitable partnership.

It is integral to your success to accommodate the needs of your potential partner as soon as you receive the green light from them. Typically, you only have one chance to attract the big boys, so make it count. Do not waste anyone's time offering theoretical partnership possibilities that are years and millions of dollars away from happening. Approach confidently with a killer deal that you can make a reality in 60 days or less. Your ability to provide your offering quickly may be the factor that tips the deal in your favor.

Mutual Non-Disclosure Agreement

Before you pitch your potential partners about your amazing product or service, send a mutual non-disclosure agreement. Why? This agreement is your protection against overreach by setting up an understanding that inhibits potential partners from taking your idea (without partnering with you!). The timing of the non-disclosure is important. Set the appointment, then send a confirmation email with the non-disclosure attached. Usually other companies are too busy working on their own growth initiatives to steal an idea, but better to be safe than sorry.

You may have to offer bigger margins/deals to make your first large partnership happen, but it will build your business, add industry buzz, and lend instant credibility. This first major partnership is known as a marquee partnership, since it is the equivalent of a brightly lit sign advertising your company. As long as you create deals that benefit your company and your bottom line, you are headed toward success. Strategic partnerships will also help you—not to mention your parents, spouse, cofounders, and any investors—sleep better at night.

Once you have exhausted your partnership opportunities with businesses with similar customers or within the same industry, it is time to think about companies who tangentially touch your customers right before they need your service or product. For example, if you are selling a baby product, you need to form relationships with OB/GYN offices, fertility tracking apps, hospitals, cord blood banks, and baby name sites. You can position yourself as a partner with an add-on benefit or product that is sold by your partner, or as an affiliate.

Another way to use partnerships with companies that precede yours in a consumer's use path is to ask what each company does with their customer information or purchased marketing lists after their key window for marketing passes. One company's junk can be another company's treasure, in that you can usually negotiate a great deal on purchasing lists that are no longer useful to a company.

For example, the wedding industry is obsessed with brides and their wedding dates, as use of most bridal services and products precede the big day. Bride contact lists are a key factor in most large wedding company's profits, so they are incredibly expensive and heavily guarded. MissNowMrs markets to newlyweds, post-wedding. When we launched, I faced the dual challenge of not being able to afford bridal lists and the fact that the women on the list were too preoccupied with dresses and caterers to respond to name change marketing by my company. Asking what some wedding websites did with their "used lists" became a goldmine for MissNowMrs.

Working with a Public Relations Firm

As you continue to push for the growth of your company, consider the use of professional public relations. A professional public relations firm can leverage their contacts within the media to generate coverage of your company. Such media coverage includes television shows, radio programs, magazines, newspapers, high profile websites, and podcasts. This type of coverage boosts awareness of your brand, hopefully driving sales of your product or service, and can provide unexpected opportunities.

When should a company consider including professional PR in their marketing mix? The answer to that question comes courtesy of Paula Conway, Founder and CEO of ASTONISH Media. Paula advises, "Businesses should include professional PR as soon as they have the finances to pay for it. If you don't have the money to sustain it, it can wait."

If you have a particularly difficult product to sell or your startup is entering a field full of large competitors, investing in early PR efforts can pay off. Often it will be important to fund a month or two of PR devoted to making you a thought leader, an individual who is recognized as one of the foremost authorities in selected areas of specialization, and establishing you as an expert. This pre-launch PR acts as a springboard for your startup launch and early promotion. Instead of grappling to establish interest and credibility as a new company, the firm can build on your previous media exposure as a thought leader as they promote your launch.

As you sell products or services to fund your company's growth, enjoy the ride. You have created something that consumers are willing to purchase. Few people can claim to have done that in their lives. Stay true to your vision as your business grows. Remember that your goal is creating a company and product or service that you are proud of, not necessarily creating a huge company.

Chapter 9 Takeaways

- Sales equal company growth.
- Sales and marketing are two very different things.
- Use strategic partnerships to grow your business and customer base.
- Used leads from a company prior to your pain point may be an inexpensive treasure.

How It Feels

Growing your business feels amazing! Much like a proud pet owner or parent, fostering the growth and improvement of your company will leave you glowing with pride and accomplishment. You will find yourself gushing about the "latest growth" to friends and family. Remember that growing is an action verb, and you, as a founder, need to be active to plan and lead your business's growth initiatives.

Every time you sell your product or service, you will feel triumphant. You have built something that consumers need and are willing to pay for! That feeling multiplies by the size of the sale or opportunity. Similarly, finding a potential partner, strategizing the best way to connect with them, and then closing a partnership deal is exhilarating. Not only do you feel a sense of accomplishment over the partnership, you also have the pleasure of knowing that you have scooped that opportunity ahead of any of your competitors.

Further Reading

Greatest Salesman In the World by Og Mandino

Little Red Book of Selling by Jeffrey Gitomer

Double Double by Cameron Herald

DO WHAT YOU HAVE TO DO
UNTIL YOU CAN DO
WHAT YOU WANT TO DO.

~ OPRAH WINFREY ~

*Elegant*ENTREPRENEUR

DELEGATE UNTIL IT HURTS

As soon as your company is operational, assess and prioritize your time for the tasks that will speed your growth and bring in dollars. Anything that you do repetitively that does not boost revenue for your business is something you should delegate. The easiest and most time consuming jobs are responding to voicemail, email, and social media; manning the front desk; labeling marketing material; and database entry.

Delegation is not as simple as it sounds. As the founder of the business, you have built your idea into a company and know exactly how to perform the day-to-day tasks that are necessary for the business to run. However, your focus should be on making the business grow. Handing over tasks to employees is hard. Make the transition easier by making a detailed set of instructions or parameters for each job. An additional step—having a one-on-one training session—will help to ensure clear communication so your business tasks will flow smoothly and consistently.

If you do not have an employee to delegate to, consider an intern or volunteer. In today's digital economy, individuals—especially students—are very eager to trade their time for work experience. Another option is to delegate to a freelancer, which you can find on Upwork (formerly oDesk and Elance). New employees, interns, or freelancers, may not answer client questions exactly the way you would, or pack product in precisely the same order, but you are freed up to concentrate on higher-level projects. And it's quite possible that your delegated tasks may be completed much faster than if you were doing them, with much less stress.

Do not allow yourself to get caught up in the "it's all up to me" mindset; it will cripple your company quickly. There is no "I" in team, especially in a startup team. Hire people whom you genuinely like and trust. You will be surprised at what a difference that makes in delegation and how once you begin to delegate it becomes easier. Be understanding that your way is not always the only way, and open your mind to the benefits your volunteer, intern, or employee brings to the company.

According to venture capitalist and serial entrepreneur Jonathon Perrelli, it is important to have an inner circle of people within your company to advise you regarding your best role within your company. This outside perspective allows you to allocate the project or job to someone else. "Winning is all that matters and you're not winning if you're in the wrong role even if you think you are supposed to be doing it," says Perrelli.

A word of wisdom when it comes to hiring friends or family members as employees: proceed with extreme caution. The boundaries of friendship and family are more delicate than you may think and the stresses of startup employee/employer roles are relentless. While friends and family members can be a tremendous source of moral support and initial help when you begin your startup, it is best to keep them off the payroll.

One scenario of things going poorly is hiring your brother, sister, or aunt into a key company role and then they do not perform well. Emotions come into play when you're stuck in a bad situation and counting on someone long term. If you keep family hires to discrete, short-term projects, such as data processing, you can benefit by having a trusted individual performing a task for you. They will benefit from some extra cash and the ability to help your company in a clearly outlined way, with a specifically defined start and end date.

The instant you introduce salaries and a new dynamic of authority into a relationship, that relationship changes. Do you want to change your relationship with one of your friends or family members? Are you completely comfortable confronting them if they are performing poorly? Do you think they will be able to separate what happens at work from what happens in your relationship? What happens if you have to fire them, or they quit?

It may be easy to picture the ideal employee in a friend or family member, but it is foolish to endanger something as beautiful as your relationship with long-term employment. Instead, solicit advice on different ideas or business thoughts from your family and friends. This is a healthy and instrumental way to enjoy their involvement and wisdom in this major facet of your life, and it protects close relationships.

Elegant Insight 9 Takeaways

- You must release lesser tasks to maintain the growth of your business (even when it is hard to let go).
- Document your methods so others can do tasks "almost" as well as you do.
- Be open to feedback and suggestions on how to improve the way things are done.

How It Feels

Delegating portions of your startup to-dos to other people feels like handing your only child to a random person on the subway. You will feel scared, paranoid, and have an intense need to hover, make lists, and check up on the individual tasked. Despite how you feel, if you have chosen a capable person and given them adequate training, the situation is not dire. Sharing tasks will free your focus and time to make your company thrive. Look at it this way: delegation equals time for high value projects plus lower stress levels.

SHE WAS UNSTOPPABLE.
NOT BECAUSE SHE DID NOT HAVE
FAILURES OR DOUBTS, BUT BECAUSE
SHE CONTINUED ON DESPITE THEM.

~ BEAU TAPLIN ~

*Elegant*ENTREPRENEUR

~Chapter 10 ~

OVERCOMING SETBACKS & COMPETITION

Setbacks are a part of startup life. No one wants their project delayed or derailed, but it happens to the best and most prepared entrepreneurs. How you choose to view and respond to your problems will be integral to your success or failure. Setbacks, viewed through the right lens, can be seen as opportunities in hiding. Fail forward, as the saying goes. You are absolutely allowed to be upset by a misfortune. Indulge in your emotions for a short period, and then use them to fuel creative thoughts and solutions for growing beyond the issue.

The ideas you generate for problem-solving may be more brilliant than your original idea, or they may open up an entirely new aspect of your business. Virtually none of the successful entrepreneurs gracing the pages of *Forbes* or *Fast Company* made it to their lofty status on a single idea that never had a problem or setback. In reality, most of them overcame multitudes of setbacks and failures before their success became a reality.

Sari Azout, Founder and CEO of Bib + Tuck, overcame many challenges building her company—a website that allows women to sell seldom-worn garments from their closets and purchase other women's seldom-worn garments (shopping without spending). After three years of continuous hustling to reach approximately 200,000 users, she successfully sold Bib + Tuck to CrossRoads. Azout shares, "Obstacles, challenges, and fears constantly evolve and change in the life of an entrepreneur. You never get to an obstacle-free zone. Accept these things as part of entrepreneurial life."

Azout cautions that fears, obstacles, and challenges get bigger as your company grows. For example, her original fear of not getting media attention for her company changed into the fear of not overcoming technology challenges to meet their launch date after a Vogue editor discovered and featured Bib + Tuck. At the time of the feature, Bib + Tuck was a minimal viable product of a landing page and short video. Her takeaway: "It becomes easier to handle obstacles as you realize they are a natural state of entrepreneurship."

Facing a setback is when grit and sheer determination come into play. The choice is yours: choose to give up and go back to your mundane 9–5 job, or choose to engage every ounce of intellect, guts, and determination to find a way to make your idea work and keep your company alive.

Merrick, Cofounder of webMethods, shares her number one takeaway from growing a $200 million company, "I've grown comfortable with risk, trying new things, and failing." She learned that disappointments and setbacks are more valuable than success. For example, when Merrick's bank account dipped down to $33 while building webMethods, it forced her to think and innovate a way to make the company profitable.

Tammy Elliot, President and CEO of Perfect Wedding Guide, shares the wisdom she has accumulated in the 11 years of growing her business in the rapidly changing print industry. "Keep your head on straight; everything doesn't go as planned in business. How you react is the difference between failure and success, and finding the detour around the setback facing you makes for a more thrilling adventure."

Weathering the Competition

Now that you have founded a business and are beginning to profit from your idea or solution, the timing is ripe for the setback of competitors reacting or new competitors popping up. It is important to know who your competitors are, and what new products they offer the instant that they appear. Setting up Google alerts for keywords pertaining to your startup (e.g., married name change service) is an easy way to stay aware. Copyscape, a free plagiarism checker, is another way to keep abreast of competitors and copycats. Their software scans the Internet for duplicate content and will alert you if another company is using your content on their website.

Know your competition. Research the company founders and any investors. Much like sizing up an opponent in a fight, you will want to know who they are, what their educational and entrepreneurial backgrounds are, and how well they are funded. Once you have the full scoop on your competitors, you can decide how best to address the situation.

If you have a service or product for purchase, it is wise to see if your new competitors purchased it from you before starting their own copycat company. Having controls in place and keeping detailed user records for your company will benefit any investigations into copycat businesses. Depending on whether you have terms of use in place (refer to Chapter 7), you may have legal recourse against the competing founders before they even get their company off the ground. Striking before the competition makes any money gives you a financial and psychological advantage. It is easier to fight for something that is making you money and covering legal fees. Competitors fighting to establish a copycat company with unknown revenue out of their own pocket or startup savings is an entirely different situation.

After I founded MissNowMrs, there were individuals who purchased my service and mined all of the forms and instructions I had spent months accumulating and creating. They essentially stole everything I had and set up a copycat service, much to my dismay. A prime irritant was the fact that they stole my startup story and passed themselves off as a couple that experienced trouble with the name-change process and then created a solution.

Within the first year of business, MissNowMrs faced the challenge of being a fledgling startup squaring off against a bully who stole my idea, story, and logo. I needed that year to focus on building my brand and making strategic partnerships to ensure the success of my company. A decision was made; I chose to fight. As the first legal battle MissNowMrs waged, I funneled entirely too much emotional energy and creativity into defending my company.

After spending tens of thousands of dollars in legal fees, and testifying in court while I was eight months pregnant, the court ruled in my favor. The competitor had to hand over their website and sign an agreement to never compete against me in the married name-change space again. Were my legal fees covered as part of the settlement? No. Was it worth the investment to defend our position as the only online name change service? Yes.

Every business is different, as is your access to funds for a legal battle. You will need to weigh the value of maintaining your company's position in the market until an honest competitor arises versus the time, money, and energy that a lawsuit will take away from your business.

Other ways to handle the appearance of new competition include acquisitions and mergers. Perhaps your competitors have one key piece of technology or a customer acquisition model that you lack. Maybe you and your competitor would benefit from joining forces and pooling resources. Therein lies the possibility that you may be able to form a partnership or purchase agreement that rewards everyone.

The silver lining is that competitors are not always bad news for entrepreneurs. Their simple existence will make you aware of your company's weaknesses or product flaws and will motivate innovation and improvement at a much faster rate. Competitors may see your customers' needs differently and provide you with the vision for a new product. They can also help expand customer awareness of your product, category, or service niche thus enlarging your potential market.

Chapter 10 Takeaways

- Setbacks are opportunities in disguise.
- Defend your company and IP immediately in copycat lawsuits.
- Competition can motivate positive change.

How It Feels

Setbacks are frustrating. When something happens that blocks your path to meeting a deadline or achieving a goal, you feel angry. Confusion about how to react or what to do next can be crippling as a founder. Failing to overcome a setback after multiple tries can leave you feeling helpless and depressed.

Learning that you have competition you were previously unaware of induces that sinking feeling of dread in the pit of your stomach. Intellectually, you know that competitors are a part of business. Emotionally the fight or flight response is triggered along with a string of questions that can easily put you into a panic. What if their product is better? What if they take all of my customers? Did they steal my idea? How do I fight them? What do I do now?

You can choose how these intense negative emotions impact you and your company. The concept of "no grit, no pearl" applies. Without a piece of sand (an irritant) an oyster would not create the protective layers that form a pearl. Similarly, setbacks and competitors "irritate" you into becoming a better entrepreneur. Each solution you devise and each competitor you defeat strengthens your mental tenacity, while at the same time builds confidence in your abilities and company.

Further Reading

The Greatest Salesman in the World, Scroll III by Og Mandino

The Resilience Factor: Seven Essential Skills For Overcoming Life's Inevitable Obstacles by Karen Reivich

THE TIME TO REPAIR
THE ROOF IS WHEN
THE SUN IS SHINING.

~ JOHN F. KENNEDY ~

*Elegant*ENTREPRENEUR

BUILD A BUSINESS SUPPORT TEAM BEFORE YOU NEED ONE

The day you receive a buyout offer or are served a company lawsuit is not the day to begin looking for a lawyer, an accountant, or an advisor for your business. Conserving startup cash is a critical factor, but not engaging qualified professionals to handle key aspects of your business to save money is foolish. Establishing a support team for your company as it is conceived is incredibly advantageous.

A knowledgeable support team—with members closely acquainted with your company, its background, vision, and end goal—is beneficial beyond measure. This team can discuss potential pitfalls or obstacles they foresee in their area of expertise, before they occur. Your company will be aptly positioned and capable of anticipating imminent threats to its livelihood. The anxiety and wasted energy your support team will prevent makes them a sound startup investment. This team can also make business connections and open doors for you.

Sourcing Business Support Team Members

Now that you understand the importance of a support team, where do you find its members? Ask other entrepreneurs for their favorite accountants, lawyers, and advisors. Also ask for personal accounts of how those professionals assisted their company. If you like what you hear, arrange for an introduction.

Another source for individuals to build your support team is local business incubators. Many incubators, local business associations, and offices of economic development have discounted deals for their participants to receive legal, financial, and advisor help. Regardless of whether you are part of the incubator, you can access their list of supporters and glean the contact information for lawyers, accountants, and mentors to interview as potential support team members.

Do not limit yourself to one professional. Take time to meet or talk with a few lawyers, accountants, and advisors. See who you "click" with and wisely decide from there. These will be the professionals you will entrust with your business and its future.

Business Lawyers

A business lawyer with experience in assisting startups and entrepreneurs is an essential member of your support team. This professional will help with your incorporation, and will also draft your operating agreement. The operating agreement is the legal document that governs how your company is run and attests how your equity is divided. Attorneys also assist with important business transactions such as partnership agreements and revenue share agreements, and they will review any offers, leases, loans, and investors to ensure you are legally covered.

Your attorney will work with you on all of the ways to protect your intellectual property and company. Such protection includes confidentiality agreements for employees, partners, and contractors. This professional will also write the terms of use which customers consent to before using your service or purchasing your product. These terms of use safeguard your intellectual property and innovations from theft by potential copycats. It is critical that they are written by your lawyer and not "borrowed" from another website or template.

If you have created innovative code or a unique process, your lawyer will help you explore the possibility of protection and assist with filing for a patent if the criteria are met. As you create your company name and logo, your business lawyer will file for a trademark to prevent other companies from masquerading as your business and stealing your customers. Registering a copyright with the United States Patent and Trademark Office is another way that your attorney can assist in safeguarding your company. The cost and time required to complete these legal processes is justified by the value of protecting yourself and your company.

Business Accountants

Finding a trusted and knowledgeable business accountant to advise you as you form your company will simplify properly setting up your accounting systems, record keeping, payroll, and tax withholdings. They can also advise you on the best way to handle incoming cash versus expenses and prepare for federal, state, and county taxes. Hiring a trusted professional to oversee your books will prevent company money from being used inappropriately and corporate credit cards from being abused. Accountants enable you to find ways to take money out of your company in the most tax efficient way. Good accountants always save you more money than the fees they charge.

Business Advisors

The final member you need to find for your team is an advisor. This should be an entrepreneur who has built and invested in several successful companies, and one who has experience in your company's field. Research founders of successful companies similar to yours and reach out to them. Start by asking a question you need to know to build your business, and then foster that relationship. When it has progressed to a level of ease, ask the entrepreneur to become your mentor. If you get turned down, ask the same question of the next entrepreneur on your list. A mentor will give you access to their experience and wisdom in startup situations to help you better launch and grow your business. They can also provide insider tips that can save you from mistakes and provide introductions to key people who can help your business.

After you have built your business support team, continue to spend time with them and keep them informed as you progress through the phases of building your business. The more you discuss your startup and work with each support team member, the easier it will be to establish trust and build a strong working relationship. These bonds become incredibly important when stressful or high priority situations occur. Trusting the advice you are given during a crisis will allow you to make informed decisions quickly. In most business situations, a fast solution can help you save money and credibility.

Elegant Insight 10 Takeaways

- Build your support team before you need it.
- A business lawyer, business accountant, and advisor are essential for startup success.
- Pick professionals you truly like and are comfortable with so you can accept their advice without hesitation.
- Build rapport with your team so you have a relationship when emergencies arise.

How Does It Feel

Researching and interviewing potential business professionals can feel daunting and tedious. It is awkward to evaluate several individuals of the same profession and then choose one that you like. You may be worried about being charged for the time you take to meet each professional. Eliminate this worry with a call or email verifying that you can do a free introductory meeting before you make an appointment.

Once you have slogged through the legwork and found the members of your business support team, you will feel an enormous sense of relief. It is like watching a safety net materialize beneath you and your company.

IF YOU ARE PERSISTANT
YOU WILL GET IT.
IF YOU ARE CONSISTANT
YOU WILL KEEP IT.

*Elegant*ENTREPRENEUR

~ Chapter 11 ~

SUSTAINING

If launching your startup was a sprint, sustaining your business is more like a marathon. As you settle into business, you will need to set a realistic work pace that you and your team can maintain for an extended period of time. There will still be late nights, but they should not be occurring on a weekly or even monthly basis.

According to Sherman, a professor for MBA programs at Georgetown University and the University of Maryland, "The sustaining phase of a business is a nice strategic plateau. You are relieved of the hyper stress of the climb to success and have time to look down on the valley you came from." He describes sustaining as "the first time in your entrepreneurial career where you are playing defense instead of offense, meaning you have built your company to the point where you can relax a little and defend what you have built."

While plateaus are pleasant, do not get too comfortable. Sherman goes on to point out that "sustaining is the stage where many businesses fail due to a lack of durability of their business model." According to the Bureau of Labor Statistics, Business Employment Dynamics Program approximately 50% of all new businesses survive five years or more and about one-third survive 10 years or more.[10]

Failure is not an option, so make sure that you are intentionally working on, not just in your business. It is easy divert attention to the daily work necessary to keep customers happy, causing you to lose sight of the big picture of planning the next steps and innovations necessary to keep your company alive and thriving. You are responsible for maintaining your vision and making sure your company reaches it, so stay focused!

Jennifer Fleiss, Cofounder and Head of Business Development for Rent the Runway, a company that provides designer dress and accessory rentals to over 5 million members, has the challenge of continuing to grow Rent the Runway beyond its current success. With the accolades of Inc. Magazine's "Top 30 Under 30," Fortune's "40 Under 40," Fast Company's "Most Influential Women in Technology," Fleiss is just the woman for the job. When asked about her tips on sustaining growth Fleiss shares, "It is a mix of staying focused on current customer satisfaction and adding new opportunities for growth." The levers she has identified for her company's growth include attracting new customers, getting deeper into their current customers' wallets, and scaling quickly. Rent the Runway recently launched an unlimited subscription that allows customers unlimited access to clothing and accessories for $139 per month. This is an excellent example of how to get current customers to spend more monthly, and thus fuel Rent the Runway's continued growth.

Invest in Yourself

One question that emerges during this phase of your company is how much to pay yourself from company profits and how much to reinvest in the company to fuel growth. This will sound counterintuitive, but you should pay yourself as little as possible. It is important to reinvest profits into company growth, technology, marketing, and your team. Think about increasing your salary when your company does not have a burning need for the next investment necessary for growth.

While you may not be able to give yourself a lavish salary, you should find ways to take some personal time away from the company. Engineer your role within your company with the flexibility to have time for what is important to you and makes you happy. Personal satisfaction and enrichment originates from assets beyond dollar signs.

Use this moment in your company's growth to invest in yourself. Join a group that focuses on supporting entrepreneurs who have moved past the initial startup phase. The Women Presidents' Organization (WPO) is an affiliation for successful female entrepreneurs worldwide, connecting women who lead multimillion-dollar companies. The WPO helps women from diverse, noncompetitive industries surround themselves with true peers. Sharing tried and true advice and experiences can fuel your company to the next level of success.

Choose to be proactive instead of reactive as a company. Positive, planned progress beats last-minute panic! For example, systematically rolling out a better user interface to boost purchases and customer engagement is better than scrambling to repair the same interface issue pointed out by angry customers or worse yet, investors.

Set weekly and monthly company goals that culminate in your annual goal for sales, product improvements, and growth. If you miss a goal, reassess to ensure the same problem doesn't sabotage future company goals.

Foster Strategic Partnerships

If you have made strategic partnerships that benefit your company, partnership fostering is important. Make time to meet your business connections at your partner's company, and ask them to involve the highest level of managers in your meeting, if at all possible. Making the effort to put your face with your company's name and build personal relationships with your partners will pay off. This is especially true when one of your competitors comes knocking on their door trying to unseat you. Ideally, the benefit of partnership fostering will come into play and your partner will refuse this hostile posturing. At a minimum, you should get a fair chance to defend your partnership before it is dissolved.

Paradigm Shifts

While striving to meet your company goals, be open to paradigm shifts—massive changes in how you see your company or see its customer base. The longer you are sustaining a business, the more chance there is for you to experience a shift in your perspective and, as a result, discover an opportunity to monetize your new vision. If you do experience a paradigm shift, remember to stay true to your vision but be versatile in exploring new business options.

Think about how to enter your market and compete successfully against yourself. How would you build a company that would crush your current one? Answering these questions will drive innovation.

You need to rethink and replace passé products before your competitors find an edge. It is easy to become attached to a product and hang onto it longer than you should. To innovate, you need to be reinventing and exploring your product or service annually.

I was standing in a Rite Aid store when I experienced my paradigm shift for MissNowMrs. For years we had been focusing on increasing the percentage of brides that purchased our service. My attention was drawn to gift cards for Foot Locker, strategically placed above the birthday cards. Nothing was placed above the wedding or engagement greeting cards section. Here was a great opportunity to expand my market! It made perfect sense because while there are 2.3 million women who get married in the United States annually, there are 230 million wedding guests looking for the perfect gift for those ladies. My paradigm shift: I saw the volume of possible MissNowMrs customers, which allowed me to build the vision of gift cards for our service in big box retail shops. A deal to place MissNowMrs gift cards in 7,000 Rite Aids was struck in 2013. Another business deal, to place gift cards in the top Target stores, was inked in July 2015. This is an example of monetizing an entirely new segment of the population, and using a paradigm shift to build new partnerships and outlets.

Business Strategy Analysis Comparison

Competitive landscape tools can also be used to pinpoint paradigm shifts for your company. They analyze challenges and create strategies for your business. Each tool has value, so select the one that aligns with your business needs and level of understanding. Two main tools explored here are the SWOT Analysis and the Porter Five Forces Analysis.

The SWOT Analysis is an analytical framework that evaluates the strengths, weaknesses, opportunities, and threats involved in a business venture. It involves specifying the objective of the business and identifying the internal factors (aspects of your company) and external factors (aspects of the environment) that are favorable and unfavorable in relation to achieving that objective.

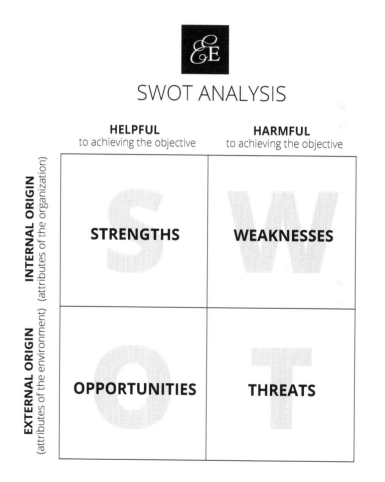

~ 171 ~

SWOT Analysis Factors

1. **Strengths:** Characteristics of your business that give it an advantage over others.
2. **Weaknesses:** Characteristics that put your business at a disadvantage relative to others.
3. **Opportunities:** Factors that your business could use to your advantage.
4. **Threats:** Factors in the environment that could cause trouble for your business.

To use the SWOT analysis to evaluate your company's position within your market, you will need to gather your team and a whiteboard to consider and list your company's internal strengths in relation to your competitors. Next, realistically list your company's internal weaknesses. Then, brainstorm a list of your external opportunities, which can stem from strengths or from eliminating a weakness. Finally, record a list of potential external threats from competitors, new government regulations, and technological changes in your industry. With all of the data categorized, you can create strategies to distinguish yourself from your competitors.

The pros of using the SWOT analysis include its simplicity and its exploration of your company from your team members' viewpoints. You do not need technical knowledge to use it effectively. Also, using the analysis allows you to capitalize on opportunities and overcome weaknesses within your company while protecting yourself from threats through the development of contingency plans (a plan designed to take a possible future circumstance into account).

Inadequate definition of factors, compiler bias in the generation of factors, lack of prioritization of factors taken into account in the analysis, and no obligation to verify aspects based on the data or analysis are all cons of using the SWOT analysis. The data you put into the SWOT analysis determine how meaningful the results are so it is imperative to avoid the garbage in/garbage out scenario. The creator of the next competitive landscape tool developed it in reaction to the SWOT analysis, which he found lacking.

The Porter Five Forces Analysis was developed by Michael E. Porter, who is the Bishop William Lawrence University Professor at the Institute for Strategy and Competitiveness at Harvard Business School. His analysis is a framework to determine the level of competition within an industry and to develop business strategies. It comprises five forces that determine the competitive intensity/attractiveness of an industry. Industry attractiveness refers to overall industry profitability. The five forces affect a company's ability to serve its customers and make a profit.

PORTER'S FIVE FORCES ANALYSIS

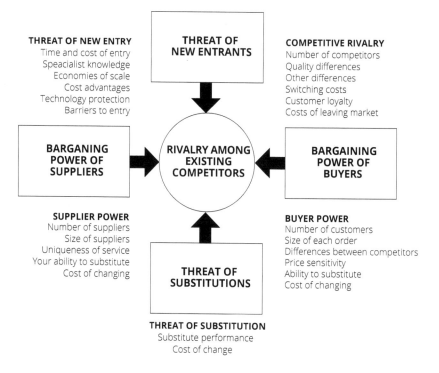

THREAT OF NEW ENTRY
Time and cost of entry
Speacialist knowledge
Economies of scale
Cost advantages
Technology protection
Barriers to entry

THREAT OF NEW ENTRANTS

COMPETITIVE RIVALRY
Number of competitors
Quality differences
Other differences
Switching costs
Customer loyalty
Costs of leaving market

BARGANING POWER OF SUPPLIERS

RIVALRY AMONG EXISTING COMPETITORS

BARGAINING POWER OF BUYERS

SUPPLIER POWER
Number of suppliers
Size of suppliers
Uniqueness of service
Your ability to substitute
Cost of changing

THREAT OF SUBSTITUTIONS

BUYER POWER
Number of customers
Size of each order
Differences between competitors
Price sensitivity
Ability to substitute
Cost of changing

THREAT OF SUBSTITUTION
Substitute performance
Cost of change

Porter Five Forces

1. **Threat of new entrants:** Profitable markets attract new companies which result in decreased profitability for all companies in the industry (including yours).

2. **Threat of substitutes:** Products or services that could replace yours increase the chances of customers switching to alternatives.

3. **Threat of established industry rivals:** The intensity of competitor rivalry is what determines the competitiveness of your industry.

4. **Bargaining power of customers (market of outputs):** The ability of customers to put your business under pressure for lower prices.

5. **Bargaining power of suppliers (market of inputs):** The ability of suppliers of raw materials, labor, or services to exert power over your company by increasing prices.

To apply the Porter Five Forces analysis to your company, begin by examining each force individually. Brainstorm a list of factors for each force and then cross reference your list with the factors on the diagram above. Then, write the key factors on the diagram and give them values ranging from 0 to 3 (0 being least favorable for your company and 3 being most favorable for your company). Total the factor values for each force and write them on the diagram. This will clearly illustrate your power in each force and you can then devise what you could change to increase your power with respect to each force.

The pros of using the Porter Five Forces analysis are numerous. You can use Porter's Five Forces to understand whether your new product or service is potentially profitable. By understanding where power lies, the theory can also be used to identify areas of company strength, to improve weaknesses within your business, and to avoid mistakes within your industry.

The cons of using the Porter Five Forces analysis include the fact that it draws upon industrial organization which can make it somewhat intimidating. Buyers, competitors, and suppliers are unrelated and do not interact, and the source of value in this analysis is the creation of barriers to entry, which are obstacles that prevent new competitors from easily entering your industry or area of business. Establishing consumer loyalty through a strong brand image and advertising is one way to form a barrier to entry for your market. For example, many businesses have tried to compete with Coca-Cola but the cost of trying to out-advertise the world's third most valuable brand is a large deterrent for new soft drink companies. Focusing on ways to block new competitors will help your business protect its current share of the market, but barriers are not a means to increase market share or grow your company.

With the elements defined by the SWOT analysis or the Porter Five Forces analysis, you can design and implement a strategy to improve your business's competitive advantage. A competitive advantage is any factor that allows your company to perform at a higher level than competitors in your market. Factors can include access to inexpensive raw materials, highly skilled professionals, or new technology that allows your company to offer a better product at a lower cost.

Warren Buffet, the most successful investor of the 20th century, coined the term "economic moat" in reference to a business's ability to maintain its competitive advantage. You have worked incredibly hard to create your product or service, so strive to protect it with the biggest economic moat possible. Also, as your market changes or new competitors appear, re-do your analysis accordingly to stay relevant and profitable.

[10.] Facts about Business Survival: https://www.sba.gov/sites/default/files/FAQ_March_2014_0.pdf

Chapter 11 Takeaways

- Startups are all-consuming at the beginning, but should regulate over time.
- Set company goals to grow proactively instead of reactively.
- Be open to paradigm shifts
- Use one or more competitive landscape tools to discover company strengths/weaknesses.
- Create and implement strategies to maintain and improve your competitive advantage.

How It Feels

There is a sense of supreme accomplishment that comes with growing a company to the point of sustainment. Your commitment to your vision created a successful business that no longer needs your attention 24/7. You now have the opportunity to invest your extra time in yourself, your family, or another idea.

Enjoying a lifestyle that is supported by your company built upon your idea makes each vacation or experience that much sweeter. You are reaping the rewards of all of your hard work! Using your experience to mentor another entrepreneur is another honor that comes at this stage of your business. You will receive endless joy, fresh perspective, and amusement by getting involved with fledgling founders.

Further Reading

Understanding Michael Porter: The Essential Guide to Competition and Strategy by Joan Magretta

The Innovator's Solution: Creating and Sustaining Successful Growth by Clayton M. Christensen & Michael E. Raynor

IF YOU DON'T SEE A CLEAR PATH
FOR WHAT YOU WANT, SOMETIMES
YOU HAVE TO MAKE IT.

~ MINDY KALING ~

*Elegant*ENTREPRENEUR

~ Elegant Insight 11 ~

LEAN IN FOR YOUR STARTUP SO YOU CAN STAND UPRIGHT FOR YOURSELF

After reading *Lean In* by Sheryl Sandberg, I found myself agreeing with many of the things she had to say about women in the workforce. Applying her initiatives to the entrepreneurial world, instead of just Corporate America, will yield faster and happier results for women in every nation. Marsha Firestone, Founder and President of the Women Presidents' Organization, holds a similar view. Firestone says, "The media consistently focuses on women in Corporate America. I do not believe that working in Corporate America is going to get us (women) where we want to go."

In my opinion, it is more beneficial for women to lean in and push to launch and grow their own company than it is to lean in for bigger roles in existing big business. We need women in top positions in all companies, but there are far fewer obstacles and stigmas to overcome when becoming CEO of a company you've founded. You will still have tremendous responsibility and pressure to succeed, but the work you do is for yourself.

Being a female founder gives you the power to make your own rules and choices without guilt or anxiety. Please realize you have the opportunity and ability to engineer your own future. You do not have to climb the corporate ladder or "jungle gym" to be successful. More and more women are shattering the glass ceilings of "big business," but if you build your own business, you can omit a ceiling of any material and then hire more women to grow with you.

Female entrepreneurs have more control over their job security and fulfillment than their corporate peers, which leads to higher levels of happiness. A study from the 2013 Global Entrepreneurship Monitor U.S. Report,[11] found that not only are women business owners ranked twice as happy as their non-entrepreneur, non-business-owner counterparts, they also have a higher level of well-being over that of men entrepreneurs. Firestone agrees, "I think women have a difficult time attaining control in their lives. Entrepreneurship is the great equalizer that allows women to have control, determine how much they make, make decisions about their working hours, and have power." Taking control of your life and job through entrepreneurship is quite possibly the best way to foster your happiness as a woman.

Merrick, Cofounder of webMethods has insights on how entrepreneurship relates to happiness. She shares, "Happiness comes from learning, growing, and doing new things. Entrepreneurship encompasses all of those." Merrick is intentionally the CEO and sole investor in her new venture, Pocket Mentor so she doesn't have to answer to anyone and is in control. Her thoughts are, "If you're leaning in for yourself and your market is stable, you have control of you." Merrick's control of her company allowed her to make the decision to delay the release of a new video series to the next quarter so she could look at colleges with her son.

Sandberg makes an excellent point that women shouldn't limit their professional aspirations in anticipation of balancing a family. I agree, and posit that they also shouldn't be afraid to use their time and talents to nurture their children as the family grows member by member. These statements are not meant to inflame or outrage; they are basic rights. The way the world of business is structured oftentimes goes against these rights and creates cognitive dissonance in working women. Sandberg is the COO of Facebook and revealed that she worried that she would lose her job and credibility by taking maternity leave. I do not believe she would have experienced that anxiety if she had founded the company.

As an entrepreneur you have choices. You can grow your company to a point where it does not need your constant attention. You can choose to hire employees to assume your duties and responsibilities while you take a break. Or you can exit your company for financial freedom or to pursue new opportunities. A break or opportunity is not just for starting a family, it can be for anything that enriches your life and makes you a better person.

One of the reasons I took the plunge into entrepreneurship was to give myself the flexibility to spend as much time being a mother as I desired. My mom gave up her career as a journalist to raise me and I am eternally grateful to her for the love, attention, and learning she poured into me. That being said, I knew when the time came I did not want to be a stay-at-home mom. But I also did not want to be a full-time working mom. I chose to build a business around my idea and then used the income and flexibility my company gave me to engineer motherhood to my specifications.

My son is my favorite startup, and I mean that in the sincerest and best possible way. I pour love, time, and energy into him every day. I cannot wait to see what amazing things he does daily and what he will do for the world someday! I am proactive; involving him with my company (currently he helps count and stack postcards for door-to-door direct mailings). Answering business questions sparked by his curiosity makes my entrepreneurial heart almost burst with pride every single time. I love that he is growing up in an environment where ideas become businesses and mamas write books on entrepreneurship.

Elegant Insight 11 Takeaways

- Working to build your company now will pay off later.
- When you are an entrepreneur, you control your paycheck, work hours, and maternity leave.
- The flexibility of entrepreneurship can help you architect your ideal life.

How It Feels

All of the stress and uncertainty that surround founding a new company are worth what you gain. Writing your own paycheck feels fantastic. You directly benefit from the effort you put into your business. Having control over your work hours adds tremendous freedom and allows you to prioritize what is important at any moment of your life.

My favorite part of being an entrepreneur is the flexibility to spend every August in Turks and Caicos with my family. I work while I am there, but I scale back my projects to focus on spending quality time with my husband and son. The experiences shared and the memories made are priceless. I come back each September refreshed with a sense of gratitude for the choices I made that allow me to live the life that I love.

[11.] Facts About Women Business Owners: http://www.babson.edu/Academics/centers/blank-center/global-research/gem/Documents/GEM%20USA%202013.pdf

EVERY END IS
A NEW BEGINNING.

*Elegant*ENTREPRENEUR

~ Chapter 12 ~

EXIT OPPORTUNITIES

Do you want to run your company forever? An even better question is: Do you see the market sustaining the growth of your company forever? Are you the best person to take this company to the next level? You may have built it to a million, but could the right person take it to a billion? Are there other ideas and opportunities that you would like to pursue, or are you content with where you are? The answers to these questions will help you understand if Chapter 11 was your last step or if exiting is next on your success path.

What exactly is an exit? The best definition of an entrepreneurial exit I have found is: *The act of freeing yourself financially.* Many times this can mean selling your company, but it can also mean generating residual income for your lifetime.

Exit Options

Reducing your role and workload, while maintaining your revenue stream, is a partial exit strategy as a founder. Automating processes and delegating large projects to competent team members can free your time to pursue other ideas and interests. Determine how much time you wish to devote to your current company and begin making the changes necessary to carve out that time in your weekly schedule. Balancing time versus opportunities can be tricky, but also very rewarding.

Mergers are another possible exit opportunity. A merger is a legal consolidation of two companies into one entity. It functions to concentrate the resources of two smaller companies into one larger company. A merger can be a difficult undertaking as duplicate positions in both companies are often whittled down to one position for the merged company. However, this restructuring typically results in lowered expenses for the merged company.

If you want to sell your company, who is your best buyer? Your best buyers are not purely financially driven. They will be the large companies that are currently operating within your industry that need something you have, or want you to go away. Buyers may also be suppliers or vendors to your current company. One of the many reasons to make strategic partnerships as your company grows is to nurture relationships that may lead to eventual acquisition.

A company is always worth what you're willing to sell it for and what someone is willing to pay you for it; but remember it is always a negotiation. There are complicated pricing models but there is no exact formula to equate what Facebook paid for Instagram. The intangibles of the synergy within your industry are what create top-dollar sales prices of your company. Instagram is a free mobile photo-sharing and social networking service that enables its users to take pictures and videos and share them on a variety of social networking platforms. In 2012 Facebook purchased Instagram for $1 billion. Why would Facebook pay such a large purchase price for a company that made 0 dollars in revenue? The answers have to do with what Facebook perceived: the value of Instagram's 30 million users, and the threat to Facebook's user base for photo sharing. Keeping other large companies, such as Google, from acquiring Instagram was also part of the purchasing equation.

Private equity firms are other potential buyers. They are investment vehicles for institutional investors or high-net-worth individuals. The investors' money is used to purchase companies. Private equity executives seek to maximize the growth of these companies' cash flow before selling them and earning an additional return for their investors. Private equity firms combine the financial resources with the corporate acumen to take your operations to the next level. Typically they retain company owners for expertise, making them an excellent exit option if you want to keep a piece of your equity stake.

An Initial Public Offering (IPO) is a type of public offering in which shares of stock in your business are usually sold to institutional investors. These investors, in turn, sell to the general public on a securities exchange. Through this process, a private company transforms into a public company; this is commonly known as "going public." IPOs are typically used by businesses to raise capital and/or monetize the investments of early private investors. A perk of IPOs is that the company selling shares is never required to repay the capital to its public investors. Disadvantages include the expense associated with the process of going public, as well as required information disclosures that could benefit your competitors.

Prepare Yourself

Perrelli, a venture capitalist and serial entrepreneur, explains that you need five people to help determine your ideal exit option and timeframe. "These five people are: a lawyer, an accountant, a financial planner, a life coach, and a therapist. When all five help you understand what you want, and what you want is offered, it is time to exit."

As you prepare yourself and your business for a potential exit, think about what your business represents to you. Your business can, and should be, both a passion and a source of income. You built and defined your business, but it does not define you. Your ideas, skills and experiences transcend your company and remain a part of you. You will continue onward and upward regardless of the sale or development of your company.

Chi, formerly of Blackboard.com and now Cofounder and CEO of WeddingWire, offers his insights on how exiting Blackboard made the founding of WeddingWire easier. He says, "As a second-time entrepreneur, being associated with a company that went public puts you in the spotlight. My reputation tied to Blackboard.com made raising money and recruiting for

WeddingWire very easy. Venture capitalists knew who I was and returned my phone calls, which made it easier to build a relationship and secure funding for my new company."

Real estate mogul, Barbara Corcoran found that her experiences building and growing The Corcoran Group made her next venture easier. She shares, "When I started on ABC's *Shark Tank*, I quickly realized that choosing the right entrepreneurs was no different than picking the right salespeople to hire at the Corcoran Group. With years of experience of picking the winners over the losers, I had an enormous leg up as an angel investor choosing the right entrepreneurs. I invested in the same people who could get over rejection and make it to the finish line."

What's Next After You Exit?

Exiting a company can result in a huge payout, and as a founder you make the monetary decisions. As women, we are subtly programmed to undervalue our work and worth, and to not focus on money. Think of the value our society places on women who are benevolent and altruistic. The media highlights women sacrificing their lives to make a difference. However, little is said of women funding companies and charities to make a difference. Women can and should strive to build and sell companies to fund their futures and finance any missions or interests that are important to them.

Julie Kirk, Director of the Office of Innovation and Entrepreneurship for the United States Department of Commerce says, "Money makes it easier for you to change the world." I could not agree more. Case in point, Kirk went on to point out that the Bill and Melinda Gates Foundation would not exist without the financial successes of Bill Gates and Warren Buffet as well as the dedication and leadership of Melinda Gates.

The Bill and Melinda Gates Foundation is committed to improving the quality of life for individuals around the world. The foundation has teamed up with international partners to take on some tough challenges: extreme poverty and poor health in developing countries, and the failures of America's education system. They focus on these issues in particular because they believe they are the biggest barriers preventing people from making the most of their lives.

Without the $28 billion donated by Bill and Melinda Gates and the 8 consecutive annual donations of $1.5 billion by Warren Buffet (which are scheduled in perpetuity), the Bill and Melinda Gates Foundation would fall short. It would not have had the resources necessary to fund their support of innovative ideas that one day might solve the challenges they have set out to overcome. The financial success of the founders and Buffet are being leveraged to make the world a better place. You now have the opportunity to leverage your financial success to improve the world.

Take time to savor the journey to your successful exit. An exit is an ending of a season in your life. Cherish the memories, friendships, and experiences that brought you to where you are today. Now is an opportune time to travel and regroup as you process upcoming changes.

An exit is also the beginning of a new season. Are you ready to generate or find another great idea and build a business around it? Your previous experiences, connections, and knowledge give you the opportunity to build smarter and faster than when you founded your first company. You also have the luxury of taking your time selecting what you want to do or build next.

No matter what form of exit you take and what good you decide to do with your earnings, you have done it; you have taken the journey of growing a company from idea to exit. Congratulations!

Chapter 12 Takeaways

- Exiting does not always mean selling your company to another business.
- Choose the exit that best aligns with your goals and happiness.
- Exits are both an ending and beginning.

How It Feels

As I have yet to experience a classic example of an exit, I gathered the reactions of others on how it feels to exit a company that you have built. The answers were poignant and all included a mention of grief.

Kirk says exiting your company feels like you have lost an appendage. She went on to say that female entrepreneurs should remember "your identity is not what you do, it is who you are."

Azout, Founder and CEO of Bib + Tuck, reflects on the sale of her company to CrossRoads, "Business takes over your life. You live and breathe it. Once you delegate it to someone else after your exit, there is a sense of nostalgia of losing something that you built from the ground up." She goes on to state that there are positives that come from selling your business, "You can cross exit off of your entrepreneurial to-do list and start in on a new idea. You can take your skills and learning into your next venture. Seeing my idea come through gave me confidence as an entrepreneur for whatever is next."

Van Pelt, Cofounder and CEO of CourseMaven examines her feelings after the sale of one of her companies. "I felt like I poured myself into the company and had given so much to it. The sale was completely transactional and it hurt. I learned that at the end of the day, a business is a business. Don't let it take over your entire life. From another perspective, selling a business is like when your kids go to college—it's exactly what you have been preparing for, but it still makes you sad."

Corcoran explains the bittersweet emotions associated with selling: "Selling a business you've built from scratch with blood sweat and tears is a life-changing experience. You feel like a mom who sold her kids to a questionable step-parent and you better be prepared to fill the space with something new."

Further Reading

Mergers and Acquisitions from A to Z by Andrew J. Sherman

DEFINE SUCCESS ON YOUR
OWN TERMS, ACHIEVE IT BY
YOUR OWN RULES, AND
BUILD A LIFE YOU'RE PROUD OF.

~ ANNE SWEENEY ~

*Elegant*ENTREPRENEUR

~ Elegant Insight 12 ~

REVIEW & REALIGN YOUR STEPS

It is human nature to have our ultimate end goal in mind and even in a photo on our desk. While it is very important to keep your goal in sight, it is also important to reassess your progress and plotted steps every 3 months.

This quarterly review schedule serves several purposes. First, it will keep you on track and motivated. Accounting for your time, as in a progress report or logged-in insert tracker, prompts you to actively drive towards accomplishing your goals. Looking back at your last 3 months, you can identify goals—steps that were connected and steps that were waylaid. Understanding the circumstances that derailed any of your steps or goals will help you avoid them the following month.

Second, the quarterly review gives you a chance to realign your next steps as the world changes. With the rapid development of technology, it may be possible to eliminate steps or it may be necessary to change course to achieve your end goal. The worst thing you can do is mindlessly follow your steps for months or even years without considering new ways to accomplish your goal. Scan the Internet for ideas and innovations related to your business. Set up Google alerts to receive daily emails on any news or articles around your goal or business niche. Consider potential partnerships or brand extensions. Follow innovators in your field on Facebook, Twitter, LinkedIn, and Instagram. The more you immerse yourself in the world of entrepreneurship and the culture around your goal, the more ideas will flow, and the faster you will achieve your end goal.

Finally, reviewing your steps quarterly can navigate directional flow of your changing life circumstances with flexibility. For instance, do you want to start a family? Or do you desire to devote more time to a loved one with an illness? Add a step in your journey. Not every step needs to be a straight line to your goal. Adding a step that allows you to experience an integral aspect of your life that may never present itself again is important. Do not lose sight of your goal, but also do not bypass significant moments in your life while in pursuit of your goal. A careful balance and quarterly reviews will keep you on track in all aspects.

What happens if your end goal changes while you are in progress? The answer is very simple: allow yourself to edit your end step. You may have spent years striving toward a particular step, but if pivoting your goal will give you more success and satisfaction, make the change. Do not enslave yourself to achieving your end step to the detriment of your happiness. Entrepreneurship is as much about an amazing and happy lifestyle as it is about the end success. Make sure that your end step will make you happy, and that the connecting steps will provide at minimum a sense of accomplishment (remember not all steps are fun). You will find as you reach your end goal or step that the journey toward success is what makes it so sweet.

Elegant Insight 12 Takeaways

- Assess your progress every 3 months.
- Add steps to allow you to enjoy significant life moments.
- Edit your steps if your goal changes.

How It Feels

Tracking your progress to your end step helps you feel in control of your life. You focus on the short-term goal to move yourself closer to your long-term goal. Having a plan allows you to begin each day with purposeful productivity and end each day with a sense of achievement.

Changing your end step can feel like failure, but it is not. Acknowledging that life and your definition of success can change will free you to prioritize your goals and attain happiness.

THE END OF THIS BOOK & THE BEGINNING OF YOUR JOURNEY

Now that you have read about the necessary steps to build an idea into a business and learned what it feels like to become an entrepreneur, it is time to apply that knowledge to your own life and idea. I know exactly how daunting that may feel, but I also know that you can do it! Let's keep the conversation going. If you have a business question that I did not cover or want to know more details on a specific step, please leave a comment for me on my blog at www.ElegantEntrepreneur.co. I am dedicated to helping you succeed as an entrepreneur!

ENTREPRENEUR &
STARTUP DIALECT GLOSSARY

One of the more embarrassing and stressful moments as a new entrepreneur is going to an event or speaking with other entrepreneurs and having zero idea of what they're talking about. Attempting to decipher the startup dialect, while making a good impression and strategic connections, does not make it easy to put your best heel forward. I remember attending a Distilled Intelligence pitch contest and sitting through 3 company pitches before realizing that "disruptive" was a positive term in the world of startups. Skim these key terms so you are confident and able to communicate when you make your industry debut.

Accelerator — A company or group that takes a small amount of equity in return for small amounts of capital and mentorship. They are typically formatted as 3- or 4-month programs.

Angel (Angel Investor) — A person who invests his or her own money into a startup in exchange for convertible debt or ownership equity. They fill the financial void between seed money from your friends and family members and formal venture capital funding.

B Corp (B Corporation) — A for-profit business dedicated to social and environmental issues.

Bootstrapping — A situation in which an entrepreneur founds and builds a company from personal finances or from the operating revenues of the new company.

C Corp (C Corporation) — A legal structure that businesses can choose to organize themselves under to limit their members' legal and financial liabilities.

Cap Table (Capitalization Table) — This table is a record of all shareholders of a company, along with their pro-rata ownership of all the securities issued by the company (equity shares, preferred shares, and options), as well as the various investments made by the shareholders for these securities. NOTE: Cap tables are very complicated and their organization and maintenance cause endless startup headaches.

Convertible Debt — A loan that can be turned into equity (stock ownership), typically upon the occurrence of future financing of the company.

Co-working Space — An office space that is shared by multiple companies to offset the costs of rent, office furniture, and equipment.

DiSC Assessment — A behavior assessment tool based on the DiSC theory of psychologist William Moulton Marston, which centers on four different behavioral traits, which are: dominance, influence, steadiness, and compliance.

Disrupter — Contrary to common use, being disruptive in your industry (by having a new idea or product that will cause big changes) is considered to be a good thing as an entrepreneur. Being labeled as a disrupter is a compliment, not an insult.

Hackathon — An event, typically lasting several days, in which a large number of people meet to engage in collaborative computer programming

Incubator — A company or group that takes equity in exchange for assisting selected startups with shared office space, office equipment, external management, advice, and industry connections.

IPO (Initial Public Offering) — A type of public offering in which shares of stock in your business are usually sold to institutional investors, who, in turn, sell to the general public on a securities exchange. Commonly known as "going public".

LLC (Limited Liability Corporation) — A corporate structure that protects the members of the company from being held personally liable for the company's debts or liabilities.

GLOSSARY

Meetup — A regular meeting of people who share a particular interest.

MVP — Short for Minimal Viable Product. This is a concept from the book Lean Startup, where you create the least portion of your service or product necessary to test its success before investing further time or money.

NDA (Non-Disclosure Agreement) — A contract in which one or more parties agree not to disclose confidential information that they have shared with each other as a necessary part of doing business together.

Ownership Equity — The owner's/founder's investment in the business minus the owner's draws or withdrawals from the business plus the net income (or minus the net loss) since the business began. Simplified, owner's equity is the amount of company assets minus the amount of liabilities.

Pitch Contest — An event that allows startups in need of seed money to pitch their company or idea to investors, receive advice from the investors, and possible funding if they win.

Pivot — A rapid shift in startup strategy to find the right customer, value proposition, and positioning.

Private Equity Firm — Firms that use their own capital or capital raised from wealthy investors to take companies private with the intent of improving them and later taking them public or selling them at a profit.

Revenue Model — A description of how a business will earn income, produce profits, and generate return on investment.

Seed Capital (Seed Round) — The initial capital used to start a new business, usually coming from the company founders' personal assets or from friends and family.

Series A Round (A Round) — The first major round of capital financing by private equity investors or venture capitalists. In private equity investing, this round is usually in the form of convertible preferred stock.

Series B Round (B Round) — The second round of capital to finance a business's growth by private equity investors or venture capitalists.

Social Enterprise — An organization that applies commercial strategies to maximize improvements in human and environmental well-being.

Stock — A type of security that conveys ownership in a company and represents a claim on part of the company's assets and earnings.

Common Stock — Stock that usually entitles the owner to vote at shareholders' meetings and to receive dividends.

Convertible Preferred Stock — Stock that includes an option for the holder to convert the preferred shares into a fixed number of common shares, typically any time after a predetermined date.

Sweat Equity — A partner's contribution to a project or to improve the company in the form of unpaid effort and toil.

UI/UX (User Interface/User Experience) — How the customer interacts with a website or product and what the experience feels like for them.

VC (Venture Capitalist) — A person who provides capital from a pooled fund (and often management and industry connections) to startups and small companies in exchange for a large portion of your business. They are willing to take big financial risks on you, because your success will allow them to sell their shares of your company for a huge profit.

Vesting Schedule — An agreement that allocates permanent company stock over a specific period of time (typically 3-5 years) to ensure that the company and cofounders are protected if someone cannot continue to contribute as originally agreed upon.

INDEX

~ A ~

~ B ~

~ C ~

Cofounder, *15, 21, 24, 39, 49-53, 55, 58-59, 61, 64-65, 69, 71, 77, 92-93, 106, 156, 168, 180, 187, 190*

Cofounders, *9, 38, 49-52, 55-56, 64-65, 69, 121, 146, 201*

CoFounderslab, *51, 105*

Competitor, *26-27, 73, 158-159, 174*

Competitors, *9, 26-28, 35-36, 39, 58, 73, 95, 109, 116, 145, 147-148, 156-159, 169-170, 172-175, 187*

Crowdfunding, *25-26, 29, 91-92*

Culture, *v, 23, 58, 61, 78, 82, 117, 135-137, 139, 193*

~ D ~

Developer, *105-106*

Developers, *105-106*

Developing, *16, 26, 40, 90, 105, 188*

Development, *8, 23, 29, 49, 57, 61, 91, 104-106, 123, 137, 162, 168, 172, 187, 193*

~ E ~

Exiting, *47, 64, 185, 187-188, 190*

Exits, *190*

~ F ~

Facebook, *24, 59, 85, 122, 124, 128, 180, 186, 193*

Funding, *v, 2, 10, 25, 29, 50, 64, 85-93, 95, 97, 99, 131, 188, 198, 200*

Fundraising, *60, 93*

~ G ~

Gauntlet, *v, 1, 3, 5-7, 9-11, 54*

Gliffy, *53-54*

Grants, *87-88, 91*

~ H ~

~ I ~

~ K ~

~ L ~

~ M ~

Platforms, *25, 40, 88, 91, 105, 107, 122, 129, 186*
Porter Five Forces, *170, 173-175*
Price, *4, 22, 25-27, 38, 86, 96, 103, 108, 114, 124-125, 127, 142, 173, 186, 210*
Pricing, *26, 96, 186*
Product, *v, 1-9, 14-15, 21-28, 31, 35-36, 38-40, 44, 49, 52, 55-56, 58-59, 61, 69-70, 73, 81, 87, 91, 95-99, 101-111, 113-116, 119, 121-127, 129-132, 142-148, 151, 156-159, 162, 169-170, 174-175, 199-201*
Products, *3, 5, 8-9, 11, 15, 25, 27, 29, 70, 80-81, 97, 103, 110-111, 131, 144, 146-147, 156, 170, 174*
Profit, *4, 22-23, 95, 104, 125, 141, 156, 173, 198, 200-201*
Profitable, *31, 41, 72, 127, 129, 142, 145, 156, 174-175*
Profits, *146, 168, 200*
Programmer, *14*
Programming, *50, 56, 106, 199*
Prototype, *101-103, 107, 111*

~ R ~

Relationships, *16, 38, 64-66, 71, 74, 89, 130, 146, 153, 169, 186*
Research, *v, 6, 8-9, 16-17, 19, 21-25, 27, 29, 55, 69-70, 74, 81, 89, 91, 96, 109, 130, 157, 163, 183*
Researching, *21, 23, 26, 165*
Revenue, *2-3, 5, 7, 37-38, 41, 51, 70, 72, 85-86, 89, 116, 141, 145, 151, 157, 162, 185-186, 200*
Revenues, *198*
Risk, *vi, 7, 10, 35, 58, 72, 123, 126, 156*
Risks, *201*

~ S ~

Sales, *vii, 9, 26, 39, 50, 60, 70, 73, 81, 86, 96, 104-105, 108, 125, 129, 132, 141-145, 147-148, 169, 186, 213*
Sales Funnel, *143-144*
Scalability, *3*
Scale, *4, 9, 14, 51, 56, 69, 88-89, 173, 183*

ACKNOWLEDGEMENTS

I am grateful and humbled by the sheer number of individuals who made Elegant Entrepreneur a reality. From family members who read and edited each iteration of the book as it progressed from a few chapters to a 50,000+ word work, to friends and colleagues who spent their precious time away from work and small children reading and refining chapters, to the inner circle of friends whose support and belief bolstered my confidence during the really hard moments: I cannot thank you enough.

A special thanks goes out to each of the amazing founders and top executives who made it a priority to share their insights and experiences, and introduced me to their favorite entrepreneurs as a way to help the next generation of entrepreneurs. They include Sari Azout, Mike Bradicich, Leslie Bradshaw, Tim Chi, Barbara Corcoran, Vanessa Dawson, Tammy Elliot, Meredith Fineman, Marsha Firestone, Jenny Fleiss, Donna Harris, Maria Izurieta, Payal Kadakia, Shahab Kavaini, Julie Lenzer Kirk, Elizabeth Kraus, Caren Merrick, Amy Millman, Lisa Morales-Hellebo, Katie Orenstein, Jonathon Perrelli, Tanya Prive, Alicia Robb, Elizabeth Scharpf, Elizabeth Shea, Andrew Sherman, Andy Smith, Elise Whang, Ingrid Vanderveldt, and Janet Van Pelt.

Each perspective, suggestion, and question asked by peer reviewers made this guide better. I owe my eternal gratitude to Shannon Allan, Stacy Callahan, Shannon Coglin, Mike Bradicich, Kevin Burow, Cindy Calland, Laura Cave, Carl Engstrom, Meghann Gould, Lynn Hull, Maria Izurieta, Eva Kanupke, Elaine Kaviani, Shahab Kaviani, Kelly J. Kelly, Nancy Kidder, Justin Leader, Amy Mitchell, Keil Oliver, Jill Padvelskis, Devin Partlow, Jonathon Perrelli, Scott Price, Pramod Raheja, Don Rowlett, Karen Rowlett, Heather Seeber, Steph Spahr, Jill Washecka, Charlene White, and Micha Wienblatt.

The professional support team that transformed my run-on sentences and stick figures into the beautiful book in your hands is world-class. Thank you to Brin Stevens, my editor, for clearing your calendar, understanding my vision and voice, being a constant source of positivity, and enduring my endless detailed ideas, emails, and questions. Thank you to Jillfrances Gray, my layout designer, for finding a way to convey elegance through the flow and feel of the text. You made it beautiful. Last, but certainly not least, thank you to Kim Smith, my graphic designer. I never cease to be amazed by how you turn an idea discussed at lunch into a tangible brand. Your endless work to perfect the cover, logo, website, quotes, business cards, and marketing materials related to this book is very evident and makes me especially proud to call such a brilliant artist one of my best friends.

Thank you to my parents for raising me to believe that I could do anything I wanted if I worked hard enough. Your unfailing love, prayers, and excellent example are a large part of who I am today. To my late grandmother, who supported every venture I attempted and whose favorite color was red: the dress worn for the cover photo of this book is in honor of your memory.

Finally, thank you to my amazing husband and son who spent many "man days" at the cabin or Home Depot to give me time to write. Culin, thank you for the endless hours of revisions, making me deal with the "big uglies," and holding my hand through this sometimes insane journey. The love, support, and enthusiasm you and Merric have shown for me and this project are what made it possible.

ABOUT THE AUTHOR

Danielle Tate is Founder and CEO of MissNowMrs.com. Prior to founding her company she was the number one sales representative for a cancer diagnostic equipment company. Her first job after college was selling Canon copiers while hiding from office building security guards. She received a BA in Biology from Western Maryland College, now McDaniel College. Tate lives outside Washington, D.C. with her husband, son, and two mischievous cats. When not writing books, running her company, and raising her family she enjoys early morning Megaformer workouts, trips to the Turks and Caicos Islands, cooking, and drinking champagne in the bathtub.

Made in the USA
Middletown, DE
04 June 2016